The Impulsive, Disorganized Child

Proven Strategies for Improving Executive Functioning Skills in Kids

The Impulsive, Disorganized Child

Solutions for Parenting Kids With Executive Functioning Difficulties

James W. Forgan, Ph.D.,
& Mary Anne Richey

PRUFROCK PRESS INC.
WACO, TEXAS

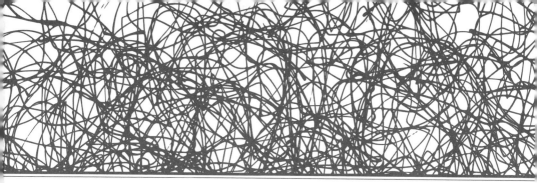

Dedication

Jim dedicates this book to his supportive family.

Mary Anne dedicates this book to her grandchildren, Maxwell and Matthew—sources of unspeakable joy—and to her husband for his tolerance, support, and great proofreading skills.

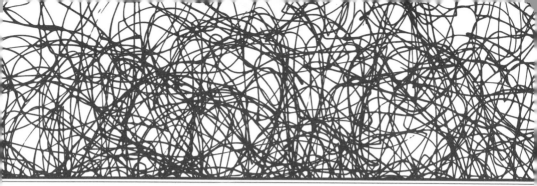

Acknowledgements

Projects like this require the work of many individuals and we'd like to thank our editor Lacy Compton at Prufrock Press for her guidance, Jodi MacNeal for her expertise, Emily Forgan for her research, and our spouses for their loving support. We are grateful to the professionals in the community who shared their expertise, especially Dr. Jill Kelderman, Ph.D., Board Certified Clinical Neuropsychologist, for her contribution on concussions in children.

Library of Congress catalog information
currently on file with the publisher.

Copyright ©2015 Prufrock Press, Inc.

Edited by Lacy Compton

Layout design by Raquel Trevino

ISBN-13: 978-1-61821-401-0

Prufrock Press Inc.
P.O. Box 8813
Waco, TX 76714-8813
Phone: (800) 998-2208
Fax: (800) 240-0333
http://www.prufrock.com

Table of Contents

Introduction xi

Chapter 1
The Big Deal About Executive Functioning.. 1

Chapter 2
General Support for Executive Functioning Difficulties..................... 17

Chapter 3
Holding Back Impulses 37

Chapter 4
Keeping Information in Working Memory... 55

Chapter 5
Shifting, Being Flexible, and Regulating Emotion............................. 79

Chapter 6
Focusing and Self-Monitoring... 101

Chapter 7
Not Just Ordinary Organizing 121

Chapter 8
Managing Time 137

Chapter 9
Taking Action 155

Chapter 10
Sustaining Effort.. 175

Chapter 11
Planning, Problem Solving, Goal Setting,
and Using Critical Thinking.. 191

Chapter 12
Children With Two Homes 209

Chapter 13
Looking Forward 221

References 231
Appendix 235
About the Authors... 257

Introduction

As parents of our own children with executive functioning difficulties, we wrote this book to provide you with information you can apply right away to help your child. Executive functioning is a broad term used to describe how the brain organizes information to help children think before acting, consider consequences, plan, organize, focus, remember, and sustain effort. (In our discussions throughout the book, we will sometimes refer to executive functioning as EF.) If your child has weak executive functions, he may be impulsive and say things without stopping to think. She may do her homework, but forget to turn it in. His or her room is a mess and completing daily tasks like brushing teeth take constant reminders. Tears are shed, and not just from your child. All of this effort leaves most parents feeling exhausted.

His or her difficulties are not just at home but also occur in school. Your child may be forgetful, easily distracted, off task, or have organizational difficulties. Your child's body is present in school but sometimes you may wonder where his or her mind is during school hours. She comes home without her assignments. Sometimes it's like he has not been taught the material because you have to reteach it. Your child's teacher recognizes the difficulties and may even ask you for suggestions.

We offer support and encouragement that you can make a long-term difference in your child's life by learning about executive functioning and being mindful of how you can help your child on a daily basis. Executive functioning is developmental in nature and providing the right kinds of intervention can improve skills. Helping children with executive functioning difficulty is multidimensional. Success is achieved with a combination of your support, teacher understanding, and your child's effort. In this book, we provide help for parents, teachers, and children in many ways, including these:

- o We offer parents strategies to help design the home environment to promote success.
- o In each chapter, there is a page of teacher strategies you can copy and give your child's teacher.
- o Your child will learn skills by relating to characters in children's books.

We want to help you help your child by engineering the environment to support your child's success. You'll find proactive steps within a three-point framework, which includes:

1. scaffolding support,
2. teaching systems of support, and
3. sustaining strengths.

This framework implies you'll help your child without enabling him or her. Your child will learn systems and routines that contribute to independence. You will build upon your child's natural strengths and talents. When a child with an executive functioning difficulty receives this type of support, he can work to fulfill his potential. We have tried to make the research on executive functioning understandable and usable while sharing our personal and professional experiences in helping children learn to approach their tasks with more purpose and confidence.

Executive functioning difficulties show up in how your children function at home, at school, in the community, as well as in social relationships—all areas we have covered in each chapter. Although there is no universal agreement on which activities of the brain are executive functions, we have chosen to cover the ones most often included:

- o holding back impulses;

- o keeping information in working memory;
- o shifting, being flexible, and regulating emotions;
- o focusing and monitoring;
- o organizing;
- o managing time;
- o taking action;
- o sustaining effort; and
- o planning (strategizing/problem solving), setting goals, and using critical thinking.

These skills are developmental in nature, so we have provided a developmental context to help you understand what to expect at various ages between 4 and 12. Of course, there can be wide ranges in development. In our work in schools, we have found that executive functioning is still a relatively new term to many teachers, even though executive functioning problems show up in many students and especially in those with disorders, such as ADHD and learning disabilities. If you suspect your child has an executive functioning weakness in a specific area, we have included a one-page reproducible sheet with suggestions you might want to share with your child's teacher in many of the chapters. Teachers are incredibly busy people these days, so we tried to make the suggestions easy to review and implement.

To give you a brief introduction of what is to come in each chapter, we have opened with a Self-Reflection Survey. After reading the chapter, we encourage you to write down an idea you can put into action. We strongly believe that one way to help children is by teaching them to use their strengths to accommodate or improve their weaknesses. To that end, we have included a section in each chapter on leveraging your child's strengths. Getting intentions down in writing is another step toward implementing them, so in the chapter entitled "Looking Forward," we provide charts for you to think about and list supports your child may need at home and school to help his or her developing executive functions. You can plan systems of support for home and school that may need to be in place for the foreseeable future as well as consider how to use your child's strengths to improve his or her overall functioning.

In our work with children during a combined 52 years, we have seen children become independent and successful. It's a process we've experienced with our own children and by working with clients. Keep in mind that this book will advise you, but if you need a guide by your side, we consult with families throughout the country. You can find us on the Internet.

CHAPTER 1

The Big Deal About Executive Functioning

"Use what talents you possess;
The woods would be very silent
If no bird sang there except
Those who sing best."—Henry Van Dyke

Self-Reflection Survey

Each self-assessment helps you reflect on your child and your parenting practices and is a preview to the chapter's content.

1. Up to this point, my knowledge about executive functioning skills is:
   a. very limited
   b. basic
   c. good but there are some gaps to fill
   d. extensive

2. Eight-year-old Jenny waits until the last minute to complete assignments. She has executive functioning difficulty with:
   a. working memory
   b. planning
   c. self-regulation
   d. processing speed

3. Sara is enthusiastic and fun to be around but she doesn't always know when she is bothering others and when it's time to tone things down. She has executive functioning difficulty with:
   a. working memory
   b. planning
   c. self-regulation
   d. time management

4. Miguel is a 6-year-old charismatic boy (his classmates call him "the president"). When he arrives in the classroom, Miguel becomes so preoccupied with talking to others that he doesn't complete his morning tasks. He has executive functioning difficulty with:
   a. self-regulation
   b. focusing
   c. goal setting
   d. inner talk

Answers: 2. b, 3. c, 4. b

Executive Functioning Skills Matter

Imagine you have a 7-year-old son, and everywhere he goes he leaves a path of destruction, as if a tornado has followed him. When he arrived home from school, his shoes were kicked off in the middle of the kitchen. His clothes were found strewn across the floor from the kitchen to his bedroom. His book bag was dropped in the middle of the hallway. And as if this were not enough, at some point he decided to make himself a peanut butter and jelly sandwich. The bread was left sitting open on the counter, the lid was off of the peanut butter jar, a sticky knife slathered with peanut butter was on the counter, and there were drips of jelly across the counter. Not to mention the jelly jar was also left open and teetering on the edge of the counter, at risk of falling over because it was left perched on top of a spoon. When you find your son watching TV, there's a sea of crumbs on the couch where he is sitting and the family dog has licked his plate clean. This boy has executive functioning difficulties.

Executive function skills matter in everyday life as we decide what is important, determine how we are going to use our time, organize our materials, stay focused on a task until it is finished, monitor our progress, and regulate our emotions. Today we live in a fast-paced, pressure-filled, and ever-changing world where people are accustomed to giving, receiving, and processing information quickly, and schools are no exception. Although rapid access to information is useful, it often creates very significant challenges for school-age children with executive functioning difficulties. A child's brain has to attend, take in all of this incoming information, decide whether it is useful, and if so, make sense of it and use it in some meaningful way.

Exactly What Is Executive Function?

There is ongoing discussion among researchers about exactly what is included in the term *executive function*. Generally speaking, it is an umbrella term for many different activities of the brain that orchestrate goal-directed action. "The term *executive skills* comes from the neuroscience literature and refers to the brain-based skills that are required for humans to *execute* or perform tasks" (Dawson & Guare, 2009, p. 13). One very simplified way to think of EF is that it is the management system of the brain. Executive function includes a person's ability to:

o   focus,
o   decide what is important,
o   set goals,
o   use prior knowledge,
o   initiate action,
o   manage time,
o   self-monitor performance,
o   use self-restraint, and
o   remain flexible.

Executive functions help modulate our attention, effort, and emotions so that we can plan, organize, and respond independently, consistently, and predictably. Having well-developed executive functions helps children regulate their behavior in social settings and their output on academic tasks.

Is There Some Agreement About What Executive Functioning Skills Are?

In our review of the literature, most authorities and researchers seem to agree EF is:

- o the brain's self-management system to organize behavior across time;
- o an umbrella term for a number of different processes critical for day-to-day functioning;
- o dependent on self-directed speech, rules, or plans;
- o goal-directed and often involves delayed gratification;
- o located primarily in the prefrontal cortex with connections to many other parts of the brain;
- o developmental in nature with some abilities showing up in the first years of life;
- o continuing to mature and develop into the teen and young adult years;
- o more critical as organizational and independent functioning demands increase;
- o impaired in many disorders, such as ADHD, learning disabilities, autism, and schizophrenia;
- o not dependent on IQ, meaning some very bright children have EF dysfunction; and
- o dependent on the situation, interest level for the task, as well as emotional/physical state.

If Executive Functions Are So Important, Why Haven't You Heard This Term Before?

It has been a term familiar to neuroscientists for decades but has become a very "hot topic" in recent years among many professionals in the fields of mental health, medicine, child development, and education. EF has been the subject of numerous studies, books, and presentations as people in disciplines of psychology, education, and neurology try to understand how deficient executive functioning skills impact children's development and ultimately their success as adults. Executive dysfunction is considered to be present in a number of disorders—ADHD, autism, schizophrenia, Obsessive-Compulsive Disorder, and dementia, to name a few, but can also occur alone. Knowledge about EF is changing the way people view and treat many of these disorders. For example, as a result of neuroimaging studies and extensive research into everyday functioning and learning, ADHD is no longer considered mainly a disruptive behavior disorder but a developmental neurological disorder related to the person's self-management system. Coaching and assisting students in managing their EF difficulty has become a part of ongoing treatment for many.

What Causes Executive Dysfunction?

Difficulty with executive functioning is caused by faulty neural circuitry and can come from a variety of causes, including genetic or environmental factors. As noted above, it is present in a number of disorders shown to have a high degree of heritability, meaning their characteristics can be passed down from parent to child in some form or another. If your child has executive functioning problems, you did not intentionally cause it, but you can do lots of things to improve your child's skills. Research has supported the plasticity of the brain and the potential for neural connections to be enhanced by experience. The purpose of this book is to teach you strategies to help any child presenting with impulsivity, poor organizational skills, weak memory, time management challenges, and other behaviors that relate to executive functioning.

EF is a very complex process involving brain structures and communication among the various regions via neural circuitry. It is not a unitary concept but involves communication and coordination among many different parts of the brain. Some executive functioning difficulties have been associated with structural/functional abnormalities in the interior prefrontal cortex. Malfunctioning synaptic connections among brain regions have also been implicated. Chronic stress, including abuse and neglect, has been shown to impact children's developing neural structures. Research and history have shown that EF difficulties can also be induced by early trauma and serious head injuries (see later section on concussions in this chapter).

> *EF is a very complex process involving brain structures and communication among the various regions via neural circuitry.*

EF skills are developmental and are thought to mature later in children with ADHD than in most others of the same age. Brown (2013) characterized the delay in development by saying,

> They are highly heritable, and they are *developmental* in the sense that they do not unfold and "come on line" at the same time ... as for most others of the same age. A number of imaging studies have demonstrated that children and adolescents with ADHD tend to show a lag of three to five years in the development of the brain infrastructure for executive functions relative to their peers. (p. 6)

Parenting styles don't directly cause executive dysfunction. However, experiences involving opportunities to learn new things, thereby creating new and strengthening existing neural connections, and structured, secure environments providing opportunities for problem solving can enhance EF. Parents who have an understanding of their children's EF difficulties can provide specific support in terms of breaking tasks down into smaller parts, providing visual supports in terms of lists, and other interventions that will be discussed at length in this book that can significantly improve functioning. Contextual variables, such as stress and illness can worsen a person's EF. Recall a time when you were under stress—more than likely your planning, focus, and decision making were not as good as they usually are. It goes without saying that children exposed to constant stress and chaos will likely have difficulty attending, regulating behavior, and being task oriented.

Perspective on Concussions From a Neuropsychologist

Parents of children, especially those involved in youth sports, frequently read or hear about concussions in the popular press and wonder about the impact on executive functioning. We asked Dr. Jill Kelderman, Board Certified Clinical Neuropsychologist, to provide her perspective on concussions and their impact on children based on her review of the most current research and her practice.

A concussion, also called a mild traumatic brain injury (mTBI), is a blow to the brain that results in loss of consciousness of less than 30 minutes, minimal amnesia surrounding the event, and mild degrees of confusion. If a student loses consciousness for less than 30 minutes, or took a hard hit and was confused and/or disoriented but was not "knocked out," he most likely sustained a concussion. A concussion can cause transient symptoms of executive dysfunction such as inattention and forgetfulness. Many people report headaches, irritability, fatigue, and feeling "foggy." In isolation, a complete recovery from a concussion is expected within days to a few weeks, although some people report symptoms lingering for up to a month, or even longer. Symptoms can actually be prolonged or worsened when children, parents, and/or coaches worry excessively about the injury. Other factors, such as preexisting anxiety or stress, have also been associated with prolonged symptoms. Indeed, psychological, social, and motivational factors are better predictors of symptom duration in concussion than the actual severity of the concussion.

There is no scientific evidence to suggest a single, uncomplicated concussion has any long-term impact on executive functioning, or any other aspect of cognition. Sports-related concussion is currently a hot topic frequently mentioned in the popular media. There is no evidence that the physical contact that occurs in youth sports causes long-term problems with cognition. The likelihood that the average high school athlete will suffer brain damage from participating in sports is extremely low. Repeated concussions over the lifespan may have the potential to lead to psychiatric and neurological problems. Additional studies are needed, however, to fully understand this relationship.

Concussion management has evolved over the years. If an individual experiences a second concussion while he or she is still recovering from an initial concussion, there is concern the injury may be more substantive, as the brain is in a state of recovery. Currently, most doctors recommend a period of rest until the individual is asymptomatic. This may involve benching an athlete for several weeks or instructing a student to stay home to rest. These decisions must be weighed, however, with the cost of missing school and/or play for an extended period of time for each individual.

Complicated mTBI involves a concussion accompanied by a skull fracture or a small bleed in the brain. These injuries are more concerning, as the blow was substantial enough to cause observable injury to brain tissue. Recovery in these instances is expected to take longer and may require greater periods of rest. In some instances, complicated mTBI in childhood poses a risk for a long-term impact on neuropsychological functioning.

If your child sustains a simple concussion, understand the expectation is for a complete recovery within days to weeks. In the interim, he or she should rest and refrain from engaging in any activity that may place him or her at risk for another blow to the head. Heavy physical activity such as running or weightlifting should be avoided. Schools can provide excused absences and accommodations with proper documentation from a physician or neuropsychologist. If several weeks have passed and your child continues to complain of headaches, difficulty concentrating, or other symptoms, and/or appears lethargic, irritable, or groggy, consultation with a neuropsychologist or sports physician is warranted. If your child sustains a complicated mTBI, he or she will be referred for a neuropsychological evaluation, which will provide specific targeted interventions as needed.

What Areas of the Brain Are Involved in Executive Functions?

To build on Brown's (2006) metaphor, the prefrontal cortex is considered to be the conductor of the brain's orchestra. Its importance was highlighted by Dr. Christopher Kye (2014) in a recent presentation as he noted,

The prefrontal cortex is the area of the brain that is the most developed evolutionarily, the latest to mature developmentally, the most complex in its neural circuitry, the most sophisticated in the cognitive functions it mediates, and the most vulnerable to dysmaturation and the developmental expression of psychiatric illness.

Advances in neuroimaging indicate that EF does not depend on the prefrontal cortex in isolation but on subcortical areas, basal ganglia, amygdala, limbic system, and the cerebellum, and on communication among synapses of various regions of the brain. (Barkley, 2012; Elliott, 2003). "Thickness of cortical tissue, global reductions of gray matter, atypical development of white matter connections across various regions of the brain, less efficient communication over white matter circuits linking various brain regions, and differences in rates of oscillations critical for linking communication from one region of the brain to another" (Brown, 2013, p. 9) have been found to impact executive functions.

Some specific EF skills have been localized to specific brain regions, but the prefrontal regions mediate the different executive functions. Patterns of connectivity and functional reorganization will be important areas of ongoing study. The scope of this book is not to discuss the neurological and physiological aspects of EF, but to provide a general understanding of what executive functions are, document that they are "real" and have been studied extensively, and help the reader understand how parents and teachers can support children with those weaknesses.

Parents, here is the good news: Your child's executive functioning skills begin developing as early as 3 to 5 months of age. However they don't fully mature until your child is in his or her 20s. The not-so-good news is that you'll need extra patience because children with deficits in executive function have been shown to lag 3 to 5 years in maturation of their neural systems, causing people to expect much more of these children than they are capable of due to their immaturity.

A young child's executive functioning skills are in a continual state of evolvement. As parents, we must continually keep this point in mind—our child's executive functioning skills are a work in progress and we must provide support. Rather than yelling at your child for forgetting his supplies, failing to start or continue working on a project, or losing his temper, try to be thoughtful and consider how you can work together to solve the problem. We can help our children by engineering their environment to enhance their executive functioning. Although poor parenting does not cause an executive functioning disorder in a child, poor parenting can make the child's executive functioning difficulty more apparent and limit opportunities for development. Significant neurological growth during the early years provides significant opportunities for enhancing your child's executive skills, as described in the next few paragraphs.

Significant neurological growth during the early years provides significant opportunities for enhancing your child's executive skills.

Initially, an infant is reacting to physiological needs but as the brain matures, he or she is able to focus attention on objects or faces, shift attention, remember faces of caregivers, and interact with the environment. Babies gradually learn to self-sooth and gain some control over their environment. "In the first 12–18 months of life, a child's working memory function is largely nonverbal in nature" (Kaufman, 2010, p. 19). This nonverbal or visual working memory enables a 12-month-old to hold images in memory for brief periods to help him or her in exhibiting some self-control. For example, a toddler may be able to recall similar incidents and results, such as being put in the crib after hitting another sibling.

The development of language provides a huge jump in the baby's influence and capability. All of us have experienced the power of a baby's "No!" Not only can infants make requests, but they sometimes mimic adult's language in an attempt to control their own behavior. This is considered to be the beginning of verbal self-regulation, which depends on a child's ability to hold information in verbal working memory to use at a later time. All of us who have worked with young children know that the development of language skills enables a child to have significantly more control over his or her behavior. Initially, toddlers and young children often direct their behavior by their verbalizations. As maturation takes place over the years, silent, self-talk begins to guide actions.

> Although verbal working memory capacity increases at about 4 years of age, children generally do not have the capacity for silent or covert self-directed speech until later in elementary school (ages 9–12). Even then, however, the ability to stop and think remains a work in progress well into the adolescent years. (Kaufman, 2010, p. 20)

In our work with children, we have seen the tremendous impact language delays have on children's behavior. The inability to articulate wants and needs can make a child feel powerless and inclined to resort to more primitive means, such as hitting, to get a desired object.

The preschool years are a period of rapid growth in brain structures and supporting networks. A significant amount of research being done at universities across the country is showing that quality preschool experiences with interactive and attentive teachers and stable home environments where parents demonstrate and model problem solving play an important role in the development of children's executive functioning. One program, The Creative Curriculum for Preschool and Teaching Strategies Gold Assessment System (http://teachingstrategies.com/assessment/research), provides opportunities for developing and assessing skills related to executive functioning in young children and is used in Head Start programs across the country. The curriculum contains specific references to developing executive functioning skills like regulating emotions, persisting on tasks, and using classification skills to aid memory. In an interview, Shelley Parker, program officer for the Children's Services Council of Palm Beach County, FL, reported increasing use of research on the development of executive functioning skills in young children to drive programming. Children's Services Council of PBC has developed and integrated a systems approach with multiple services and programs to increase the quality of the preschool experience both in the family and in preschools. The Council funds agencies using evidence-based programs designed to enhance the interaction between teacher and child and uses the Quality Rating Improvement System to monitor and coach teachers. If you have a preschool-aged child, check out your local area or preschool for proactive stances on executive functioning development in young children. Preschool is not just babysitting and play without a purpose anymore!

Two Theoretical Models of Executive Function

There is no one universally accepted theory of executive function. For the purposes of this book, we have utilized primarily the theories of Dr. Russell Barkley and Dr. Thomas E. Brown, both of whom have studied and written extensively on a number of childhood disorders and EF. They have both proposed their own theoretical models of executive functioning with some key differences. Although this may be more information than many of you need in order to implement strategies outlined in this book, it highlights the depth of work being done by researchers in the field.

Barkley (2012) defined executive functioning as "those self-directed actions needed to choose goals and to create, enact, and sustain actions toward those goals usually in the context of others often relying on social and cultural means" (p. 176). He agreed with many other theorists that self-regulation is a key feature of EF. However, he suggested that areas of self-interest including emotion, self-awareness, and motivation are often overlooked in discussion of EF. He made the point that two individuals could choose entirely different courses of action based on their assessment of whether an action is worth the effort when weighing their current state against their future happiness. Barkley pointed to a social and cultural aspect at the highest level of functioning, noting that cooperation with others can facilitate reaching goals that could not be attained alone and culture impacts choices one makes. In his "Extended Phenotype" model of EF, he classified some routine, automatic, self-regulatory functions as "pre-executive," including attention, memory, as well as primary emotions and motivations.

In Brown's model of executive functioning, he described how the executive functions work together to help people accomplish tasks. Brown's (2005) model includes the areas of:

- *activation*: organizing, prioritizing, and activating to work;
- *focus*: focusing, sustaining, and shifting attention to tasks;
- *effort*: regulating alertness, sustaining effort, and processing speed;
- *emotion*: managing frustration and modulating emotions;
- *memory*: utilizing working memory and accessing recall; and
- *action*: monitoring and self-regulating action.

Brown (2006) encouraged us to think of effective executive function like we would the conductor of a symphony skillfully bringing together components of a performance. There are many different parts that have to come together to produce the desired effect, just as many different executive functions have to engage for a child to be successful. As he wrote,

> Regardless of how well the musicians in a symphony orchestra may play their instruments, they are not likely to produce very good symphonic music if they do not have a conductor to select what piece is to be played, to start their playing together, to keep them on time, to modulate the pace and volume of each section, and to introduce or fade out various instruments at appropriate times. Although each musician may play his or her instrument skillfully, the subtle, dynamic, integrated functioning of the orchestra depends crucially upon the coordinating and managing functions of the conductor. (p. 37)

Frequently, a child's mother plays the role of the conductor or executive organizer. Although moms are willing to help their child out, it leaves them feeling worn out, frustrated, and wondering, "What is wrong with my child that he or she can't manage him or herself?"

Parents often describe their children with weak executive functioning skills as lazy, unmotivated, disorganized, scattered, impulsive, careless, and frustrating. In many ways, this is far from reality, because youth with EF difficulties often work as hard as or harder than those without EF difficulties. Structural and functional delays in brain development, as well as differences in neural networks, have been documented that indicate children's failure to perform is not willful disregard for responsibilities. If a child has difficulty with executive functioning, he or she will have to expend more energy to pay attention and get tasks completed. It is important to take a critical look at the child's strengths and weaknesses to determine where supports are needed.

> *Structural and functional delays in brain development, as well as differences in neural networks, have been documented that indicate children's failure to perform is not willful disregard for responsibilities.*

How Are Executive Functioning Difficulties Formally Evaluated?

Executive functioning involves the interplay of many different areas of the brain and is very dependent on the context of the situation and many factors intrinsic to the child, making it very difficult to evaluate. The fact that there is no consensus definition of executive function further complicates the matter. In fact, executive functioning difficulties are not recognized as a formal diagnosis in the *Diagnostic and Statistical Manual of Mental Disorders* (5th edition; DSM-5), which psychologists and doctors use to make formal diagnoses. Nevertheless, executive functioning difficulties are real and are important to assess.

There are a variety of tests that evaluate specific executive skills, including the Stroop Task, the Wisconsin Card Sorting Test,

Auditory Attention, Inhibition, and the Trail-making Test, which can provide some valuable information. These tests are usually administered by psychologists in a quiet, controlled environment and are of short duration. Neuropsychologists can gain valuable insight from the NEPSY–II, which can include information about attention and executive functioning, language, visuospatial skills, and sensorimotor functioning. One caveat is that the examiner provides structure and specific directions, so the outcome may show deficits in the test scores but the scores may not provide a clear picture of how a child would manage independently in the complexity of a busy school or home environment. An astute psychologist will provide the link of how the low scores may appear as behaviors in the classroom.

There are also rating scales designed to measure executive functioning, which can also provide valuable information. Some of the concerns that exist around the various rating scales, like the Behavior Rating Inventory of Executive Function and the Barkley Functional Impairment Scale–Children and Adolescents, have to do with the subjectivity of the rater. A comprehensive evaluation would include the specific EF tests, rating scales, a psychoeducational or neuropsychological evaluation, as well as observations and interviews of the student, parent(s), and teacher(s). The results from an evaluation may help you identify specific areas of weakness and then provide targeted support.

Next Steps

After reading the overview about executive functioning, we hope you have gleaned some helpful information that you can put to use in your child's life. We find that ideas communicated in writing have a much better chance of being executed. Take a minute for the following exercise.

An idea I can put into action is . . .

_____

_____

_____

_____

_____

_____

_____

_____

_____

_____

_____

_____

_____

_____

_____

_____

CHAPTER 2

General Support for Executive Functioning Difficulties

"The secret of change is to focus all of your energy, not on fighting the old, but on building the new."—Socrates

Self-Reflection Survey

1. My executive functioning skills are not as important as my child's executive functioning skills.
   a. true   b. false

2. The term *scaffolding of skills* means:
   a. building something with my child
   b. teaching my child something
   c. provide temporary supports as my child's executive functioning skills evolve
   d. identifying the skills my child lacks so I can teach those skills

17

3. When I think about my child, he or she has more executive functioning weaknesses than strengths.
   a. true   b. false

4. I have information about executive functioning that I can give to my child's teacher(s) so they have a better understanding of how to help my child.
   a. true   b. false

Answer: 2. c.

General Support for EF

Now that you have a general understanding of executive functions, what are you to do to help your child? In each chapter, we provide targeted information about strengthening specific executive functioning skills broken down according to age—whether younger or older children—as well as to the setting—home, school, or community. There are several general strategies that are basic to managing all EF difficulties: We recommend helping your child develop adequate executive functioning skills by providing three key components:

1. scaffolding of skills,
2. teaching systems of support, and
3. sustaining strengths.

Scaffolding of Skills

Scaffolding of skills means that you will need to provide *temporary* supports as your child's executive functioning skills evolve. Scaffolding is a term many teachers use to explain how they support students during learning. For example, a teacher may begin writing instruction by providing a prompt such as a picture or starter sentence. This support helps the child get started. Once the teacher sees the child has mastered how to start writing, she removes the prompt and allows the student to start his or her own story.

Let's suppose your first grader frequently calls out during instruction. The teacher may place a visual reminder, such as a stop sign, on your child's desk. This provides a temporary support to remind your child not to call out. Or the teacher may place a tally sheet on your child's desk. Each time your child calls out, the teacher instructs your child to make a tally mark on the sheet. This increases your child's

Scaffolding of skills means that you will need to provide temporary supports as your child's executive functioning skills evolve.

awareness of how often he calls out. The teacher would remove the tally sheet when your child's call outs decrease to an acceptable level. This type of teaching encourages independence.

The temporary support is just enough to help your child master the skill. As parents, we strive to help our children become independent and self-sufficient beings. By scaffolding support, you are teaching your child to exert effort within a safe environment to help himself. The child must be on board and willing to participate in learning and changing his or her behavior. You may wonder, "Why wouldn't kids get involved?" It is often due to anxiety, failure, or internal feelings of "why try?" As parents, it is important not to continually do things for your child if he or she has the skills. Although it's often easier for a parent to do the task, it's sending the wrong message and your child is missing out on learning a valuable lesson about work and effort.

If the child does not have the skills necessary for completing the task, temporary supports have been shown to be very instrumental in helping with skill development. Parents scaffold support when they use a sticker chart to help their child learn to monitor his or her own behavior. The chart is a temporary external support that is used to help the child recognize when he or she is meeting the expected behavior. Jim used a chart like this with his kindergarten age son. One target behavior was, "Use nice words." Jim and his son talked about examples of nice and naughty words. Jim set expectations that his son would use nice words. Then, throughout the day, Jim's son was verbally reinforced for using nice words and at the end of the day, he earned a sticker for using nice words. This charting system was a temporary support, used for 2 months, and then removed because the behavior improved.

Systems of Support

Systems of support help executive functioning weaknesses and are typically of longer duration than scaffold support and may even follow a child to college. As you've provided temporary support, you may have also helped your child develop a sustainable system that functions as a tool so he or she can complete the skill independently. Jerry was known in his home for always forgetting to brush his hair and teeth. His mom scaffolded instruction with visual notes reminding him of the steps. She paired these with her verbal directions. As Jerry became better at remembering, she gradually stopped the verbal directions and just left the steps posted on his bathroom mirror—a system of support. One day, when she was cleaning the mirror, she noticed the steps were missing (found under the cabinet) and were never replaced. It was then she realized Jerry had internalized the steps and was completing them on his own.

However, sometimes systems of support, like visual reminders or organizational tools, need to remain in place for the long term. College students with disabilities consider the disabilities coordinator at their college to be an invaluable system of support. Even adults seek support from life coaches. Think of systems of support you rely on in your own life to facilitate your functioning and which systems might benefit your child.

Sustaining Strengths

Sustaining your child's strengths helps your child feel confident and successful. Consider the adults you know. Do most adults have careers in their area of strength? The person who is good with numbers may be a financial planner or accountant. The people person may be in sales. A person with good hands may be a surgeon, carpenter, athlete, or mechanic. Most people naturally gravitate toward a career where they have talent. We believe your child's natural talents will carry him or her through in life—so you don't want to spend so much time, energy, and effort on the weaknesses that you overlook the strengths.

Jim talked to a dad who said it this way, "If my son spent as much time on his schoolwork as he does playing Minecraft, he'd be doing great in school." This dad recognized that what you spend your time on shapes your future. At the time, Jim's son, who has executive functioning difficulty, was 12 and also highly interested in Minecraft, so he and Jim discussed how he could take that passion and use it to make some money. After researching, they discovered Jim's son could have his own Minecraft server, set up a donation portal, and other players could donate money to have certain privileges. So, with some time and money, that's just what they did—during one month, Jim's son earned $300 in donations! This experience helped Jim's son spark a deeper interest in web and graphic design, so that when he entered high school, he enrolled in the Information Technology magnet program.

How can you harness your child's natural strengths? For most parents, it's a combination of time, energy, and research. First, you need to make time to really understand your child's strengths. This is not always easy. If you're in a negative cycle with your child and he or she is on your last nerve, then ask a relative, teacher, or close friend to describe your child's strengths. Next, gradually invest energy into your child's strengths. Most children with EF difficulty easily get overwhelmed, so teach in small chunks. Give your child just enough information to pique his or her interest but not enough to send him or her into shock.

Third, spend time doing research to match your child's interest to possible activities. In your mind's eye, fast forward to when your child has graduated high school. Do you see your child attending college or entering the workforce? Regardless of how you picture your child, he or she will need to select a college major, seek technical training, or begin employment. Do you recall the once popular catchphrase, "Do what you love and love what you do"? What does your child naturally love that could serve as a way to become independent and self-supporting? Does your child love bugs, nature, people, design, fashion, the human body, building, exercising, or arguing the law? Provide your child with experiences or even volunteer work where he or she can try out the skills by shadowing others.

As a caveat learned from Jim's personal and professional experience, use judicious judgment before investing significant money into building your child's passion. Many children with EF difficulty become very passionate about a topic or interest while it has newness and novelty but when that wears off, drop it like yesterday's news. Feelings of resentment may occur if you're left with expensive items and no one using them. Jim worked with one family whose teenage son became passionate about baseball, swore up and down that it was his high school sport, and convinced his family to spend nearly a thousand dollars on high tech baseball bats, a glove, training tools, and clothes. Unfortunately a few months later, the son decided baseball was not all he anticipated, so he finished the season and, much to his parents chagrin, found a new passion in racing radio-controlled cars. After this experience, the boy's parents required him to save his own money to buy a radio-controlled car.

The moral of the story is to consider spending as much effort building your child's strengths as you do trying to correct his or her weaknesses because ultimately, strengths sustain. Your child's natural strengths will endure and may provide a way for him or her to bypass the executive functioning difficulty. Can you relate?

Recognizing Your Own EF Strengths and Weaknesses

As parents, we each have a profile of executive functioning strengths and weaknesses and most of us learn to leverage our strengths to help work around our weaker areas. Consider the parent who wants to contribute but has very poor time management skills. This parent has great intentions, so she volunteers as room parent even though she constantly runs late. The teacher quickly learns that despite her intentions to help in the class, she will arrive late for all activities including reading to students, chaperoning field trips, and bringing goodies for the fall festival party 30 minutes after it started. This parent may leverage her strength of being motivated to help others with a caring and generous heart by using technology to set her watch 20 minutes ahead of time or set audible reminders. You can harness your strengths to help circumvent your weaknesses.

Harnessing Your Parenting Strengths

We can harness our parenting strengths to help ourselves and our children. In order to help our children improve their executive functioning skills, it's often helpful for us, as adults, to recognize where we have executive functioning strengths and weaknesses. Take a few minutes and honestly consider yourself. Take the survey in Figure 1 by placing an X in the box for each area so you can identify your own strengths and weaknesses.

Now that you've considered yourself, where do you have strengths? What are your weaknesses? We believe it is important for you to understand this because, for example, if you recognize your own weakness in time management, you may not be the best person to help your child learn time management skills. You may need to either: (a) shore up this area in yourself first, (b) ask a family member or close friend to help, or (c) enlist the help of a professional coach, counselor, or teacher.

Considering Your Child's Executive Functioning Skills

Now consider your child's executive functioning skills as you complete the assessment in Figure 2 with him or her in mind. In what areas does he or she have strengths and weaknesses? Do your child's weaker areas match your weaker areas? If the answer is yes, can you both work on the area or do you need to use a strategy or technology to bypass the area?

John, a highly successful financial advisor, was an intelligent man who quickly could keep abreast of the pulse of the market, assess a client's need, gather the big picture, analyze risk, and make informed

Parents' Executive Functioning Skills

Directions: Place an X in the box for each area so you can identify your own strengths and weaknesses.

Area	Weaker 1	2	3	4	5	6	7	8	9	Stronger 10
Holding Back Impulses										
Memory										
Flexible Thinking										
Focusing										
Organizing										
Time Management										
Taking Action										
Self-Motivation										
Goal Setting										

Figure 1. Parents' executive functioning skills assessment.

Your Child's Executive Functioning Skills

Directions: Place an X in the box for each area as it relates to your child's strengths and weaknesses.

Area	Weaker 1	2	3	4	5	6	7	8	9	Stronger 10
Holding Back Impulses										
Memory										
Flexible Thinking										
Focusing										
Organizing										
Time Management										
Taking Action										
Self-Motivation										
Goal Setting										

Figure 2. Your child's executive functioning skills assessment.

decisions. His gifts helped him become a highly sought after advisor. His weaker area was in fulfilling the minute details of paperwork. Knowing this, rather than frustrating himself and his clients, he employed a staff member to take care of the paperwork, scheduling, and other needs. This small cost allowed him to maximize his talent of helping others make money.

When John's fourth-grade son was diagnosed with ADHD, John and his wife understood the relationship between time management, organization, and school success so they swiftly hired an ADHD coach because this was neither parent's forte. The coach taught John's son how to organize his materials as well as estimate the time needed to complete assignments.

Electronics and Executive Functioning

Undoubtedly, electronics have improved many facets of our lives, but they also create challenges for many children, especially older ones, with EF difficulties. Have you noticed at your local mall how many young children have smartphones? Any time there is down time, people are on their screens. If you've ever picked your child up from school, it's easy to see how many young children have smartphones and immediately go on them as soon as school ends. Even in restaurants, we sadly see families on their devices rather than communicating across the table.

Many children, especially those with EF difficulties, have difficulty screening out distractions. If they are allowed to leave their cell phone on while doing homework—which we strongly discourage—the phone can alert them every few minutes about their friends' activities. Very little information can go into long-term memory with constant disruptions. If your child has a phone, having strict rules about its availability during study time will be important.

Another problem with children on Internet-connected devices is the potential for inappropriate accidental exposure. Many kids with EF difficulties act impulsively without stopping to think of the consequences of their actions online. With any electronic media, parental oversight is crucial these days because of the danger of predators, cyberbullying, and the inappropriate content available on the web. Unfortunately there are websites that try to tease or lure unsuspecting viewers on a whim, allowing access to inappropriate material. Establish family rules for use of social media, discuss potential dangers, and keep lines of communication open about social media. Make sure you have adequate parental control filtering software and/or tracking programs on all devices and have access to online communications and review them frequently. This is one task you can't put off until tomorrow. If you don't have adequate parental controls, address this issue today, because it only takes seconds for your child to have exposure to negative content.

It will also be important to add restrictions on purchases that can be made via the Internet or within apps. It is very easy for an impulsive child to click the "yes" icon to buy an item without first checking with his or her parents. We probably all know parents who have been shocked when viewing their credit card statements to find purchases inadvertently made by their children.

On the other hand, using technology for educational purposes can be very helpful. Most children with EF difficulties are wiped out by the end of the school day and view more pencil and paper work at home to reinforce skills as cruel and unnecessary punishment. Many apps provide skill practice in fun ways. Not only do they hold the child's interest, they also provide immediate reinforcement and practice. Reading or doing math on the computer or tablet can be much more appealing. Of course, activities like those aren't a replacement for the homework that must be turned in the next day. Other worthwhile tools are digital flashcards, which are available as apps and can result in improved recall of information. Organizational and motivational tools available electronically can make a huge difference for children with EF difficulties. You can have digital sticky notes, such as the app Post-it Plus, or make reward charts and keep track of "to-do" lists through apps such as Todoist, Epic Win, or iReward Chart.

Executive Functioning in the Home

We've explained executive functioning skills using the examples of how an orchestra's conductor keeps everyone on track. What about home? If you are the executive organizer of your household, you're likely exhausted. If you have a spouse, your spouse needs to know that keeping a child or children with executive functioning difficulties on track can be a full-time job. If you are a single parent, it's even harder to manage a child with executive functioning difficulty. Having efficient systems of support is more important than ever. We encourage you to establish routines that become automatic so everyone knows what to do and follows through. Well-established routines help minimize your child's executive functioning difficulty, as well as reduce stress.

How Strong Executive Functioning Skills Present in the Home

Juan is an 8-year-old boy who lives with his single mother, Rosa. On the weekend Rosa enjoys sleeping in, but Juan is typically awake and out of bed by 6 a.m. She taught Juan the skills and routine so that when he wakes up, he gets out of bed and goes to the family area where he can turn on the television. She leaves it set to his favorite channel, but also taught Juan how to find his second favorite channel. Rosa sets out his box of cereal, a bowl, and spoon the night before. She taught Juan how to pour the cereal into his bowl as well as how to get milk from the refrigerator and pour it onto his cereal. Juan even knows to return the milk to the refrigerator after he pours it. Rosa scaffolded the skill instruction until Juan had a solid system in place to follow his morning routine. She used his strength of being trustworthy to stay in the home watching television until she got out of bed. This extra sleep helps her recharge from the frantic workweek. Do you have such well-established routines?

Additional examples of strong executive functioning skills parents may see in the home include:

o   Taking off dirty clothes and placing them in the clothes basket.
o   Putting away folded, clean clothes into drawers.
o   Feeding a pet.

- o Taking out the trash without arguing.
- o Setting the table when asked for the first time.
- o Brushing teeth without being nagged.
- o Organizing materials in a backpack the night before school.
- o Bringing his or her own plate from the table to the sink.
- o Scraping food scraps in the garbage can before placing the plate in the sink.

How Weak Executive Functioning Skills Present in the Home

- o He goes to bathroom but doesn't flush.
- o You tell her what to get from her room and she forgets the direction.
- o She does her homework but forgets to put it in her folder or backpack.
- o He frequently melts down when things don't go his way.
- o She gets out the door in the morning rushed and filled with stress.
- o He can't pick out his own clothes to wear.
- o The floor in her room is covered with clothes, books, and toys.
- o She gets out supplies to cook but rarely puts them away.

For example, Kim scaffolded skills when 8-year-old Samantha could not get herself ready to leave for school in the morning without the stress of running late and Kim's continual nagging to keep her on track. Kim identified that Samantha had difficulty with dressing because she was sensitive to the texture of her clothes so she put clothes on and took them off until she located what felt right. Kim did not pick out Samantha's clothes but rather had Samantha try on her next day's clothes the evening before so that when she dressed in the morning she knew the clothes felt fine.

Executive Functioning in School

Undoubtedly, strong executive functioning skills help children achieve school success. Teachers have long recognized the importance of a student's ability to be prepared, organized, and attentive. As we have noted, EF skills develop over time as the child matures. The demands on a child's EF system increase with each grade. Many children with executive functioning difficulty can function fine in the early elementary grades because the teacher provides so much external support. As the demands increase in higher grades, their deficits become more apparent and problematic.

> *Many children with executive functioning difficulty can function fine in the early elementary grades because the teacher provides so much external support. As the demands increase in higher grades, their deficits become more apparent and problematic.*

How Strong Executive Functioning Skills Present in School

- o   He has a sharpened pencil when it is time to work.
- o   She turns in her homework without a reminder.
- o   He listens and focuses when the teacher is providing important information.
- o   He can keep several mathematical operations in mind while solving math problems.
- o   He can transition between different tasks with minimal or no reminders.
- o   He can glean important insights from a story he is reading because he can keep different kinds of information in mind.
- o   He can refrain from blurting out in the classroom.

Even though he is only a kindergartener, Latavion enters his classroom on time, greets his teacher, unpacks his backpack, and then places it in his cubby. In the first few weeks of school, he mastered the classroom routine. He sits down at his desk and promptly begins his morning work—writing in his journal. When a classmate tries to distract him by showing a toy he brought from home, Latavion looks at it with interest but picks up where he left off with his journal writing. When the reading block begins, he gets out his book, goes to the proper small group, and begins reading. Yes—he is a teacher's dream!

How Weak Executive Functioning Skills Present in School

- The child does not follow the morning routine and comes into class and then wanders around instead of putting away his or her backpack materials.
- The child doesn't start on "bell ringer" morning work.
- During instruction, the child is unaware of the correct page she should be on in the workbook.
- He does not know where his pencil is or she doesn't have a sharp pencil.
- After teacher instruction, he dilly-dallies around instead of getting to work.
- She appears to listen but does not remember.
- The teacher tells the child to go get a book and he returns with a game.
- She is unaware she is the last one ready to line up.
- Teacher gives instruction and when done, the student says, "What do we do?"
- He is easily irritated when another student touches his desk.
- He digs at his eraser and creates a pile of eraser debris on his desk.
- He tears at papers inside his desk.
- She chews on her own shirt and winds up with a wet collar.
- He loses his paper or pencil.
- She leaves parts of her lunch on the lunch table.
- He repeatedly calls out in class.
- He frequently slides out of his seat.
- She touches others while standing in line.
- He interrupts the teacher.

o   He uses a loud voice inside the classroom.

o   He makes inappropriate body noises.

o   She rarely completes class work within the assigned time.

Janie, a 6-year-old kindergarten student, is very social and loves to be around people. She has no problem talking to children her own age, older children, and adults. When Janie arrives in her classroom in the morning, she would rather talk with other kids than put her belongings away. Her teacher is constantly redirecting her to stop talking and to empty her backpack into her cubby. She starts putting her materials away but quickly becomes distracted and wanders away from the cubby area, and her teacher frequently takes her by the hand back to the cubby and waits with her until her backpack is empty. Furthermore, her homework never gets turned in unless the teacher gets it out of the backpack herself or nags her to do it until she gets it done.

When it is time to start learning, Janie does not have her needed materials. When she does have her materials, her pencil is usually not sharpened so she gets out of her seat to sharpen it. While doing this, she misses instruction. Janie's teacher is frustrated with her lack of focus and has tried to assign her a student buddy and move her seat. Although these interventions helped some, Janie is still having difficulty in the classroom. At this point, Janie's learning has not suffered, but her teacher is concerned about first grade. Janie has difficulty with organization and focusing and will require more support to be successful.

Providing Information to Your Child's Teacher About EF Skills

Most teachers want to help kids with executive functioning difficulty and will try the strategies they have learned to do so. The challenge for most general education teachers is they have not received much formal training on helping children with EF difficulties. In each following chapter, we provided a reproducible strategies page that you may give your child's teacher.

Executive Functioning in the Community

Your child is full of vim and vigor. He is active, aware, and busy but may be too preoccupied to listen to directions during a sports game. She has friends and enjoys interacting with people but struggles with controlling her emotions when things don't go her way. Your child's executive functioning skills play a large role in how he or she functions in the community. Some children operate much better in the community because they are able to be more active and don't have as many cognitive demands as they do at school. Other children have more trouble functioning in the community than in structured home and school environments because the community is unstructured and can be unpredictable. This is especially true for children with behavioral control issues. Nevertheless, the community is a good place for your child to practice and refine many EF skills—planning an outing, remembering the schedule for the day, being flexible when plans don't work out, and persevering with a job until it is complete. If children struggle with academic tasks, it is also a great place for them to uncover new passions and make new friends.

How Strong Executive Functioning Skills Present in the Community

- o   She brings the toys needed to the play date.
- o   He remains level-headed when he strikes out in baseball.
- o   He uses words instead of fists when he is upset at a friend.
- o   She does not immediately cry when the activity does not go her way.
- o   Rather than pointing and loudly yelling, he whispers to you, "That man only has one leg."
- o   He does not throw a tantrum when told you won't buy any candy in the check-out lane.
- o   When eating in a restaurant, he sits for an age-appropriate time.
- o   Rather than just staring at all of the choices, she makes a decisive decision about the color of nail polish to use.

o   At church, she tunes into the lesson and even raises a hand to answer a question.

Jesse was a 10-year-old whose passion was playing ice hockey. He meticulously took care of all his equipment but especially his hockey skates. After each practice, Jesse dried his skates and put on skate guards. When he got home, he took his skates out of his bag, took out the insoles, and wiped down the skate again. He took off the skate guards so moisture did not build up in them and air-dried the entire skate. Jesse had a place for all of his hockey equipment and had very strong organizational skills.

How Weak Executive Functioning Skills Present in the Community

o   He butts into other kids' play.
o   She gets into other kids' personal space.
o   He runs about when it's not appropriate.
o   She appears to listen but does not remember.

Jolene had been begging and begging her mother to allow her to join the local Brownie troop. She bounded into her first meeting and was thrilled to see the girls were having a snack. She quickly grabbed a plate and several cookies, completely missing the direction that each girl was to have only one cookie. She started horseplay with another girl before finishing her snack, inadvertently turning over her juice. When the girls were called over to discuss the project for the evening, Jolene went willingly but was quickly irritated because another girl took the seat she had wanted. The leader intervened and guided Jolene to another seat. The craft for the day looked like a fun one, making cards for a local nursing home, but Jolene hadn't remembered the directions and needed additional instructions and organizational assistance from the leader. Luckily, the leader had made a step-by-step guide with visuals that Jolene was able to follow.

The leader was able to identify a peer to help Jolene learn the procedures for the troop meeting. The girl was older, so Jolene looked up to her and happily followed her lead. The leader recognized Jolene's need for structure and always provided her with a visual of what the finished project should look like, as well as step-by-step directions with visuals. Furthermore, the leader recognized Jolene's enthusiasm and was able to use that as a means to motivate other troop members and also to help Jolene feel like a contributing member to the troop.

Next Steps

In this chapter, you processed a lot of information. What did you learn about general strategies for improving executive functioning skills that you did not know before reading this chapter? Before you forget the great thoughts swirling around in your mind, consider making a few notes below about your next steps.

An idea I can put into action is . . .

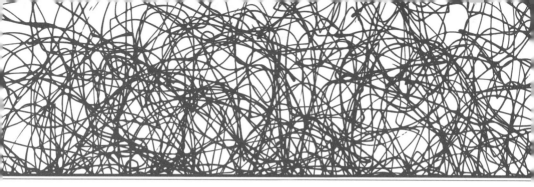

CHAPTER 3

Holding Back Impulses

"It's not about being the best. It's about being better than you were yesterday."—Unknown

Self-Reflection Survey

1. My child hits his siblings or friends and/or calls them names:
   a. often; it's a regular problem
   b. sometimes
   c. rarely or never

2. At school, my child gets in trouble or requires disciplinary action:
   a. once a day or more
   b. once a week
   c. once a month
   d. rarely or never

3. Does your child engage in any of the following behaviors?
   a. runs ahead of the group
   b. likes to climb on things and jump off
   c. takes other children's possessions
   d. has a very difficult time sitting still or being quiet
   e. all of the above

4. In our home, when one person is speaking,
   a. everyone else is speaking, too—it's always noisy
   b. the speaker is often interrupted
   c. everyone is allowed to finish what he or she is saying

5. In our home, we have clearly defined rules and expectations for behavior, and our child(ren) know(s) what's expected.
   a. yes, always
   b. sometimes
   c. no or rarely

Is This a Problem?

How do you know if your child has difficulty holding back impulses? If the behaviors listed below describe your child, you are in the right chapter.

o   Interrupts frequently
o   Moves constantly
o   Says things without thinking
o   Engages in name-calling
o   Hits impulsively
o   Melts down quickly and/or cries
o   Must have wants/needs met immediately or causes a disturbance
o   Tries to run from you when upset
o   Frustrates easily
o   Tears, breaks, or throws things when mad
o   Yells at others when upset

If your child's executive functioning challenges manifest as difficulty with impulsiveness, consider these strategies to help at home, in school, and in the community.

What Is Impulse Control?

You can think of impulse control in a couple of ways. One is that it's a big, red stop sign, keeping a person from behaving or acting in a rash and thoughtless manner. It's that moment to stop, think, consider, weigh other options, and make sure it's safe and wise to go ahead. Kids without well-developed impulse control skills just keep running the stop sign—because they don't see it. For them, it just isn't there. Can you imagine what it would be like to drive without any clue when and whether you're supposed to stop and yield to other cars? That's how it may be for your child.

Another way is to think of impulse control is as your own personal Jiminy Cricket. Remember him from the Disney animation of the children's classic, *Pinocchio*? Pinocchio was a wooden puppet, hand-made by a loving craftsman who wished it could turn into a real boy, so great was his longing for a son. When the puppet does magically come to life, Jiminy Cricket acts as his conscience. He talks Pinocchio through the consequences of his actions and gives pretty wise advice (for a cricket). Why did Pinocchio need Jiminy Cricket? Because he didn't have any life experience. He was brand new at everything, and he didn't have a clue why he should or shouldn't do things. Jiminy Cricket tries to help out, and even though Pinocchio makes a series of pretty boneheaded decisions, his little voice of reason is faithful. It may be that you need to serve as your child's Jiminy Cricket for a while longer. Eventually, with your guidance, he'll start to connect his impulsiveness with its consequences and with its effect on the people around him.

The ability to hold back impulses is a key building block to other executive functioning skills. It requires the person to assess a number of variables very quickly:

o   Do I need to respond to this stimulation/situation?

o   If I need to respond, what is the appropriate response?

o   When do I need to respond? Right now? In 5 minutes? Tomorrow?

o   How do I expect my planned response will affect the people around me?

o   Do I have enough information to respond, or should I find out more or ask more questions?

o   Is this situation making me feel emotional? In what way? How does that emotion affect what I'm about to do?

There's an awful lot that goes into holding back impulses. As you work with your child, it's important to remember that *no one is born knowing how to do it.* In a way, impulse control is like being required to do dozens of simultaneous calculations in your head, almost every moment of the day. But instead of getting numbers for answers, you get appropriate behaviors and actions. It's a lot of work.

Developmental Context

As we know from observing our children throughout their development, self-discipline in the form of inhibitory control starts developing gradually toward the middle to the end of a child's first year. It gradually increases as understanding and language skills develop. In fact, language is one of the key elements in acquiring impulse control. You'll often hear a young child talking aloud to herself about what she's supposed to do or not supposed to do. "I'm mad at you, Dolly.

> *Language is one of the key elements in acquiring impulse control.*

I can't get your dress on right. I want to throw you. Would that hurt you? That might hurt you. That might break you. I won't throw you, Dolly. I love you."

There is some consensus that true self-control is evident at 2 years of age, when many children can comply with adult directives (Campbell, 1990). If you look at the example of the little girl frustrated by her inability to dress her doll, you didn't need to tell her not to get angry and throw the toy. She has developed the ability to act without your instruction. "The basis of self-regulation is the child's growing awareness of the desire to act and the feelings that are engendered by this desire; the child becomes guided by these feelings" (Teeter, 1998,

Table 1. Guidelines for Impulse Control Development

4–5 years	■ "Can delay eating a treat; . . . can keep an arbitrary rule in mind and follow it to produce a response that differs from their natural instinct" (Center on the Developing Child, 2014, p. 9)
6–9 years	■ Are more internal in thinking and more adept at controlling momentary impulses
10–12 years	■ Become more flexible in thinking and able to switch between a central focus like driving and peripheral stimuli that may need attention, such as pedestrians (Center on the Developing Child, 2014)

p. 65). The next part of impulse control comes when the child is able to have that conversation with herself, internally. Barkley (1997) has noted that "behavioral inhibition and nonverbal working memory systems arise earliest in child development" (p. 210) with internalization of speech or verbal working memory coming later.

The general guidelines in Table 1 were compiled from information from the Center on the Developing Child at Harvard University (2011), as well as research from Barkley (1997) and Teeter (1998) about what to expect at different ages.

As we all know, some children are much more pliable than others—likely caused by differences in temperament, frustration tolerance, environment, and relationships with authority figures. And some children struggle simply because their brains have not developed as quickly as the brains of their peers. Children with ADHD, for example, are known to have developmental lags in their skill sets—meaning that their abilities in some areas may lag 2–3 years behind peers of their same chronological age. Barkley (1997) has found in his research that "impulsiveness is associated with a greater delay in the internalization of speech" (p. 282). In other words, children—especially those with hyperactivity—are not as effective as others in using self-talk or internal dialogue to guide their behavior.

Inhibition can also be impacted by a child's ability to problem solve or shift the way he or she is thinking about a problem. Inhibition has been proven to be a very complex process—much harder than just refraining from doing something. It requires the development of working memory and what is called "interference control"—the ability to keep unimportant information from playing into the decision-making process (Barkley, 1997, p. 210). Working memory enables a child to recall similar situations and outcomes, think of consequences, and consider potential rewards. It stands to reason that the ability to keep these kinds of information in memory helps a child make good choices.

How does a child's brain prepare itself to make those good choices? One of the features in the development of the brain's frontal lobe— where much of executive functioning is seated—is a process called *myelination*. Myelin is a fatty sheath that serves to insulate the bundles of axons that connect different areas of the brain (Dawson & Guare, 2010). This insulation helps improve the brain's processing speed, with development continuing into the mid-20s.

The brain's neural connections—what we call gray matter—typically develop in a different way, with a spike in growth that peaks around age 5, followed by a gradual reduction of unnecessary or unused connections. Another period of rapid growth takes place at around age 11 or 12, again followed by another round in which unused connections are lost (Dawson & Guare, 2010, p. 3). In fact, according to research by the National Institutes of Mental Health (2011),

> Scientists believe that the loss of synapses as a child matures is part of the process by which the brain becomes more efficient. Although genes play a role in the decline in synapses, animal research has shown that experience also shapes the decline. Synapses "exercised" by experience survive and are strengthened, while others are pruned away. (para. 11)

This suggests that after about age 5, and again after about age 12, areas that aren't utilized begin to diminish. To us, this means that children with EF difficulties may be at particular risk to lose the very neural connections they need for executive functioning. Put another way, it's important to continue to help our children flex their muscles in areas like impulse control, organization, and memory even if we don't see immediate results. You've heard the saying "use it or lose it." We don't want your child's neural connections that guide executive functioning to wither away from lack of use.

Let's take a look at some practical ways you can teach, support, and encourage your child.

In the Home

Maybe you know a child like Ethan who has embarrassed his family by loudly commenting that a person is fat or funny looking. At the mall one day, Ethan loudly announced that the cashier checking them out talked funny because her tongue was pierced and then asked why she had a big hole in her ear (it was from a gauge earring). Ethan's dad has learned a quick apology usually helps in these awkward situations. Although Ethan is only 9, his dad secretly wonders how Ethan will function in the working world as an adult. Have you had these worries?

Your kid is getting on your last nerve. We've been there. Of all the executive functions, the lack of impulse control in a child can be the single most irritating. See if this sounds familiar: You're trying to have a telephone conversation, but your daughter yells out every 30 seconds or so with some (to you) meaningless comment or question. And when she's not interrupting you, she's bouncing a Superball off the ceiling, trying to hit the blades of the ceiling fan. While singing. Loudly. The same song. Over and over. Off-key.

You've told her plenty of times not to interrupt you while you're in the middle of a conversation, whether it's on the phone or in person. You've established a family rule that no one's permitted to throw balls in the house. You've mentioned that you enjoy her singing, to a point. How often do you have to say it?

The answer? A lot. While your other children learned to control themselves after a handful of reminders, your child with EF difficulties may need dozens. Or hundreds. We suggest you approach each incident as if it is the very first, remembering that it is going to take a ton of practice for him or her to understand all of the complex processes that go into self-control.

Here is a bit of bad news for parents: You may be the partial cause of your child's impulse control difficulties. Researcher Roy Baumeister and colleagues (2007) reported that when parents had vague, conflicting, or no house rules, kids with impulse control difficulty have a harder time managing their impulses. It turns out that when parents specify and agree on consistent rules, consequences, and expectations, it helps a child self-regulate better. Kids know what to expect and have the predictability and structure that is comforting because they understand their boundaries. The good news for parents is that if you don't already have house rules, you can still develop them and help your child with impulse control difficulty.

Helping Younger Children at Home

More often than not, the goal is to help younger children stop doing something. Stop hitting your sister. Stop interrupting. Stop running off when we're in the store. That impulse is not yet hard-wired, and so you and your child may find a visual symbol helpful. What if you put a big, red stop sign prominently in your family room or your kitchen? Then, when the child has acted impulsively, you smile, point to the sign, and issue a calm reminder to take a moment to think before acting.

Popular children's games also can be a big help teaching younger children the ability to stop, wait, or follow instructions. Think of Red Light, Green Light. The goal of the game is to be the first to cross the finish line, but you're called out if you move on the red light. The child with impulse control challenges will have to work harder to stop at the proper times, but it's great practice. Simon Says and Follow the Leader are games that help develop a young child's ability to pay attention and follow directions. And we know a secret: Although it's fun to play these kinds of games at school, it's even more fun to play them with Mom, Dad, Grandma, or Grandpa.

Providing structure can help you keep your discipline consistent and your routine the same. When kids know what to expect, there is less chaos and less opportunity for impulsivity. Also, be sure to teach listening skills. Sometimes kids behave impulsively because they don't listen to the directions. Before finishing a sentence, they are up and moving without really hearing what is said. Teach children to listen to the directions first by having them repeat back what they've heard before they take action.

You'll be pleased to learn that giving children age-appropriate chores can help children with impulse control difficulty. Strayhorn (2002) explained how household chores help young children learn compliance, which in turn teaches self-regulation and impulse control. If a parent gives the command for a child to turn off the video game system, the child practices compliance, but a child practices self-control when a child complies with his own internal voice that says, "Turn off the system so you don't get in trouble." You can gradually influence your child so as he completes chores, he relies less on your direction and takes more initiative.

Helping 8–12-Year-Olds at Home

We've already learned that by this age, children typically will have mastered the concept of internalized dialogue—a lightning-fast review of their options and of the consequences of certain behaviors before they act. But your child probably still needs help talking through that split-second between the impulse and the action or behavior.

We suggest that you spend a minute breaking down the thought process you want to model for your child. Let's say your child has become frustrated with a homework assignment, and angrily ripped his paper to shreds. Now, of course, he's crying because he knows he's going to be in trouble for destroying his worksheet. The point of your focus isn't the destroyed worksheet—you'll take care of that later, with the teacher, even if there's a consequence for missing homework. Your focus in that moment is to help your child see how he can talk through the situation on his own: "I don't get this homework. It's too hard. And I've erased so many times I made a hole in the paper. I want to rip it up. But if I rip it up, I won't be able to finish it. I'll get a bad grade. My teacher may be upset with me. Maybe I should ask for help. Maybe I need to take a break." The idea is that you want your child to see there are a lot of options beyond his initial instincts.

Also, set clear expectations for behavior and be willing to enforce them consistently. If your child has a problem interrupting you, decide how you want her to indicate she needs you, and how long she'll be asked to wait. In one family, when an adult was on the telephone and a child needed to interrupt, she was asked to come and touch her parent on the arm. The parent would hold up a finger, acknowledging the request and indicating it would be just one minute. The trick? Make sure you make it no more than a minute before you disengage from your conversation and turn your attention to your child. It's frustrating for anyone to be told, "Just a minute," and then be made to wait 10 minutes. Everybody needs to play by the rules. Also, be sure to thank your child for her patience. In doing so, you recognize that she has just made a major step in what is a very difficult skill for her.

Books for Children

Children enjoy being read to, and in this chapter, and others, we include recommended books you can read with your child. You can use books to help teach your child executive functioning and problem solving skills. As you read to your child, follow this framework:
1. Read the book ahead of time to make sure it's appropriate.
2. Read to or with your child and pause to discuss the book's ideas.
3. Discuss how the book's character used the skill or solved a problem.
4. Discuss how the book's concepts can help within your family or at school.

The books below are available online or in major bookstores.
o *Sitting Still Like a Frog: Mindfulness Exercises for Kids (and Their Parents)* by Eline Snel, for ages 5–12
o *Mindful Monkey, Happy Panda* by Lauren Alderfer, for ages 4–8
o *Take the Time: Mindfulness for Kids* by Maud Roegiers, for ages 6 and older
o *My Mouth Is a Volcano!* by Julia Cook, for ages 4 and older

○ *Learning to Feel Good and Stay Cool: Emotional Regulation Tools for Kids With AD/HD* by Judith Glasser and Kathleen G. Nadeau, for ages 9–12

At School

Your child's school day probably is very structured. This helps his teachers maintain order, but it also makes the child with impulse control difficulties stand out like a sore thumb. He is also surrounded by other children who still may be learning self-control, and he may react to them in impulsive ways. It's likely he speaks out of turn, has a hard time sharing, or responds physically to another child if he's accidentally touched or jostled in line or in gym class.

We suggest parents and teachers introduce what we call "incompatible behaviors" to help a child learn how to master his own impulses. The first step is to identify the trigger. Notice precisely when the impulsive behavior happens. Then design a solution that physically prevents the child from acting on the impulse. Here are a couple of examples:

○ If your child has a problem calling out in the classroom, suggest that she sit with a pencil or pen gently pressed against her closed lips. This will serve as a physical reminder not to blurt out an answer or speak out of turn.

○ If your child has a hard time keeping her hands to himself when he's in line, remind him to walk with his hands clasped or in his pockets. It will be much harder to hit another child if his hands aren't free.

When students act out, it's often because they're frustrated on some level with their executive functioning difficulty. They may feel like they're not as smart as the other kids (though it's unlikely this is true). Rather than be perceived as a dummy, they'd rather be viewed as the class clown. In their minds, it's better to look like a behavior problem than to look stupid. Consider Mike. His dad says he is like a boy without a filter. Anything that is on his mind comes out of his mouth, so needless to say, Mike is considered a talker. His excessive talking gets him into trouble in school because Mike talks out of turn while his teacher is teaching, when he is working in groups with other students, and while standing in line. During lunch, the lunch monitor frequently warns him and finally becomes so fed up she tells him to sit on the stage. Mike told his dad he feels embarrassed, but there's little he can do.

Children who act impulsively often struggle to make and keep friends, at any age. Remember, they haven't yet developed the ability to consider the consequences of an action, including how it may make others feel. We encourage teachers and parents to let younger children have a "do-over" to teach appropriate behaviors, rather than simply punishing the impulsive behavior.

You can suggest the following strategies to your child's teacher, or try them at home:

o   Plan fun, engaging lessons that include puppets, songs, and stories to discuss emotions and feelings. Students learn from stories about characters who struggle with the same emotions and can relate to the characters' experiences.

o   Use strategies such as self-talk to empower a child to work through emotions without reacting on them. When a child encounters a situation that leads to negative emotions, provide words to help the child work through the situation by naming the emotion and give solutions for dealing with the problem.

o   Have the student work with a specialist on therapeutic exercises to inhibit impulsivity.

o   Make the child feel that the he and his teacher are a team. Use questions like, "How can we make this easier to understand?" Don't make the child feel like he is "the problem."

o   Be aware of triggers and warning signs that may cause the child emotional regulation difficulties. The teacher may therefore minimize precursors that can affect the child's behavior.

Suggestions for Teachers

Deficits in executive functioning, like poor impulse control, can significantly impact children in the classroom. We wanted to offer some suggestions that might help improve classroom functioning.

- o   Make teaching impulse control a class activity. Consider purchasing the book, *Impulse Control Activities and Worksheets for Elementary Students* by Tonia Caselman.

- o   In the classroom, provide visual aids to help children learn to stop, reflect, and respond.

- o   Use the "think aloud" procedure to help children learn to develop and understand their inner voice.

- o   Give students opportunity for purposeful movement such as stretch breaks or playing a class round of Simon Says.

- o   Notice students using impulse control and have a brief, on-the-spot teaching moment to explain how the student used impulse control. Discuss how this applies to others.

- o   Develop a "cue" that's just between you and the student with impulse control issues. For example, if you notice your student isn't listening to directions, you might catch his eye and touch your ear as a subtle reminder.

- o   Prepare students ahead of time for situations where they will need to apply a lot of impulse control. For example, if the class is going to listen to a guest speaker in the auditorium, tell students they will be expected to sit and listen quietly. Ask students to choose seats next to classmates who won't tempt them to goof around.

- o   Become aware of the times that students have the most impulse control difficulties, and build strategies and solutions specific to both the student and the circumstance.

Suggestions for Teachers, continued

o   Often, students with impulse management challenges have difficulty with transitions and change. It's wise to give your class plenty of advance notice if there will be a major change in your daily routine.

o   Young children will follow your lead on how to deal with a student who is struggling with challenging behavior. The teacher sets the tone for building a respectful classroom community where children feel comfortable discussing their thoughts and feelings.

o   Students with impulse control issues often feel like the bad guys, because their behavior so often lands them in trouble with you. They may feel like you don't like them. Even if you don't like their behavior, find ways to let them know that you're on their side.

In the Community

Challenges with impulse-control can affect your child's safety. A young child who acts impulsively can run out into a busy street or crowded shopping mall, without regard for the dangers or the whereabouts of his parents. Older children may take much greater physical risks, lacking the comprehension that serious injury can occur. We're not writing about teens in this book, but teenagers who are unable to challenge their impulses are at much greater risk for drug and alcohol addiction, sexual experimentation, binge eating, or irresponsible spending. We can't stress how important it is be consistent in helping your child understand all of the possible outcomes of his actions while he's young, for his own sake.

It's almost as if one of your primary parenting jobs is to continually teach your child how to stop and think, and to consider the consequences of his actions. When appropriate, use a "think aloud" procedure to verbalize your own thoughts as you consider adult situations that require you to stop and think. Next time you are eating dinner as a family, explain to your child, "I was in a meeting today and one of my coworkers gave the dumbest idea. I almost said aloud, 'That is the dumbest idea I've ever heard.' Thankfully I stopped myself, and kept my thought to myself. If I'd said it aloud, it would have hurt his feelings and made the boss think I was not a team player. In school, have you ever *almost* said something that would have gotten you in trouble?"

There's also the social component to impulse control issues. More than any other executive function issue, delays in self-control masquerade as poor behavior. Researchers at Harvard University's Center for the Developing Child found that

> children who have problems staying focused and resisting urges to act impulsively—two core executive functioning skills—not only have trouble in school but also have trouble following directions generally and are at elevated risk of displaying aggressive and confrontational behavior with adults and other chil-

dren. (Center on the Developing Child at Harvard University, 2011, p. 5)

It's easy to see that kids with self-control issues could have trouble with their peers, but it's going to affect their relationships with the adults in their lives, too.

Therefore you must prepare your child well in advance. Role-play possible situations where you anticipate there could be problems. When Jim and his family visited cousins, they always had a talk beforehand to explain expectations. They talked through how their elementary-age kids could respond if they had a problem. The conversation went like this: "We expect the two of you to get along with your cousins and not argue. If there is a problem, walk away. It's better to walk away without saying anything and solve the problem later, after you've had time to think about it, rather than saying something that will get you in trouble. Last time you all argued about the video games. This time, we will set a timer so each person knows when his or her turn playing the video game is over. Your cousin may not stop when her turn is up. What will you do if she is not taking turns? Right. Ask nicely and if she doesn't stop, you let me know."

Leveraging Strengths

Sometimes, impulse control difficulties manifest themselves more in certain areas or circumstances, and those areas tend to become your primary focus. It's only natural—you want your child to learn and grow in the situations that are the most troubling. Often it's those areas we call attention to, pointing out what she did "wrong" and the ways she needs to improve. We'd suggest another approach. As a 4- and 5-year-old, Jim's son had little inhibition, which made him an expert tree climber because he had no fear of heights, but he was able to recognize dangerous situations that exceeded his climbing abilities. Karen, a parent of 12-year-old Monroe, said, "In ice hockey he's a natural because he just reacts and doesn't look." We challenge you to find at least one area in which your child seems to have managed an age-appropriate level of impulse control, and let that be the example that guides the rest of her behavior in this area.

For example, let's say your 6-year-old daughter exhibits most of the classic signs of impulse control difficulties, but you've noticed that for whatever reason, she does have the ability to stop herself from eating too many cookies or too many pieces of candy at a time. Maybe food just isn't that interesting to her. Every time she shows restraint in this area, you can congratulate her for showing impulse control. Then, walk her through the mental processes she's not even aware went into the decision. Her self-talk could have gone something like this: "There's a big plate of cookies. I've already eaten two. Do I want any more? Not really. Why? Because I'm not hungry. Or because there are lots of other people in the room, and maybe they want some. Or because they were pretty gross cookies."

The key is to clue her in to the self-talk that led her to limit her own behavior, whatever the reason. It's much more powerful to see how she's done it effectively than to have her weaknesses pointed out to her again and again. When you show her an example of a time she has successfully curbed her impulses and it's worked out well for her, she starts to put together the pieces of how it all works. She starts to understand the essential elements, and with enough awareness and practice, she'll be able to duplicate the process.

Leveraging Technology

In most chapters, we recommend technology usage to help children with EF difficulties. But in this chapter, we recommend you limit your child's screen time to 30 minutes per day. Allowing children instant access to information and social media promotes distraction and impulsiveness. Older children (and adults) may feel they are missing out if they don't check their social networks. So even while they're studying or doing homework, they're also impulsively checking their social status. Thus, children are not learning how to sustain attention, which is so important for effective studying. There are programs you can use to block older children from websites so they can't impulsively check Facebook, Instagram, or Twitter when they should be studying.

Next Steps

After reading this chapter, take a minute for the following exercise.

An idea I can put into action is . . .

_____

_____

_____

_____

_____

_____

_____

_____

_____

_____

_____

_____

_____

_____

_____

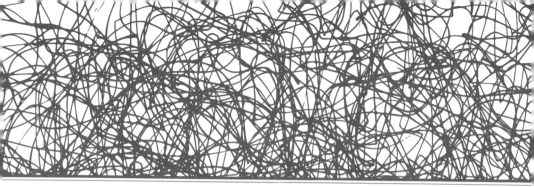

CHAPTER 4
Keeping Information in Working Memory

"There are no failures. Just experiences and your reactions to them."—Tom Krause

Self-Reflection Survey

1. Working memory is:
   a. recall of distant events
   b. ability to remember dates and facts
   c. holding information in memory temporarily while using it to complete a task

Deficits in working memory can cause children to forget directions in the middle of a task and to fail to remember consequences of past actions. If you think your child has not learned from previous mistakes, poor working memory could be at fault. When an incident occurs, he may not be able to call up details about a similar incident to guide him in handling the current situation effectively. If a child is poorly organized, she might not be able to remember where her belongings were left. Working memory deficits can also cause children to lose sight of steps to reach a goal or to even forget what the goal is—it's frustrating for all involved. As you can see, working memory is critical for completing tasks and making good decisions.

One fifth-grade girl describes her difficulty with working memory as, "It's like the information is in there but swirling around like a tornado and I can't find the right information I need. It's like all the math information is in there and then someone hit the delete key and it disappeared." It goes without saying that working memory problems are very frustrating for children, their parents, and their teachers.

How many times have you stopped in the middle of what you were doing to remind yourself of what you started out to do so you can plan your next step? If so, you were using working memory. Or if you have been stopped by a policeman for speeding several times, your working memory would allow you to pull previous instances from long-term storage to be used to inform your response—pull over to a safe spot, locate your license and vehicle registrations, etc.

If you are interested in a more in-depth discussion of memory in general, Russell Barkley breaks it down into nonverbal and verbal working memory. He describes *nonverbal working memory* as recall of the sensory representations of an event as well as the response and outcome of the event. *Verbal working memory* has been called "internalization of speech" or "self-directed speech" (Barkley, 1997, p. 175). The individual is able to verbally label events, think about responses, and consider various responses. Ideally, it results in using internal self-talk to regulate behavior. To tie verbal and nonverbal memory together, Baddeley (1986) has described three components of the working memory system: (1) visual-spatial sketchpad holding and using visual and spatial material, (2) phonological loop containing verbal information, and (3) central executive coordinating both verbal and nonverbal working memory.

Working memory can be closely related to overall cognitive ability, but many very intelligent people have weak working memory, as we know from the humorous example of the absent-minded professor. Unfortunately, many people with weak working memory also have poor organizational skills, so the load placed on their working memory is even greater. Joey, for example, had no system for organizing materials he needed for school each day. Therefore, in the morning, he had to remember what he needed for school and where he had put his jacket, backpack, and lunchbox. When his mother helped him establish an organizational system, his jacket and backpack were always by the door, which significantly reduced the load on his working memory.

Working memory in its more sophisticated form is related to creativity. Tools of the Mind is a research-based program with a developmental curriculum for early childhood used in many preschools and kindergartens, both public and private. It focuses on the development of many executive functions related to early school success, like working memory. The organization's website stated that working memory "makes it possible to reflect on one's thinking (meta-cognition) and is critical to one's ability to see connections between seemingly unconnected things, which is the essence of creativity" (Tools of the Mind, 2014, para. 8, Glossary section). Its website, http://www.toolsofthemind.org, offers wonderful play activities for parents.

Developmental Context

Barkley (1997) has noted that "behavioral inhibition and nonverbal working memory systems arise earliest in child development" (p. 210) with internalization of speech or verbal working memory coming later. He projects that verbal working memory does not likely contribute to working memory tasks below the age of 3. As you would expect, memory improves with the development of language skills. As with all skills that are developmental in nature, there can be wide variation in skills that would be considered to be within a normal range.

Another important factor in memory is the child's ability to prevent distractions and irrelevant information from interfering with learning. As we have noted before, attention and focus are critical for memory and learning.

Most young children are not developmentally ready to use strategies to remember information but depend on prompting and repeated presentation of the information or action over time. Teeter (1998) has noted that when 3-year-olds begin to apply some memory strategies, their strategies are often ineffective but become increasingly better with age. It is very important to provide a stimulating environment with access to opportunities to experience new things as a way of improving your child's memory. By expanding exposure, you give children greater context for classifying information. It has been proven that "cultural and environmental conditions can either help or impede the development of memory strategies" (Teeter, 1998, p. 122).

Another important factor in memory is the child's ability to prevent distractions and irrelevant information from interfering with learning. As we have noted before, attention and focus are critical for memory and learning.

Table 2 gives some general developmental guidelines of what to expect at different ages as working memory develops.

In the Home

In our busy lives, it is very easy to become frustrated when your child needs constant reminders and repetition of information and directions. With all of the things on your to-do list, you may mentally check off a task you have asked your child to do, only to come back later and find that the job has been forgotten. Before getting too upset, it is important to analyze what has taken place. First of all, you need to make sure that your child is hearing and processing what you are saying. One way to check this out is to ask him to repeat your request.

Table 2. Guidelines for Working Memory Development

3 years	■ Can keep two rules in mind and act on them
3 1/2 years	■ Can use past knowledge to help them remember (Wellman, Somerville, & Haake, 1979)
5 years	■ Begin to recall location of items, such as in a memory game or by finding items in a room
7 years	■ Can begin to use simple memory strategies, like organization of material, but usually need prompting (Teeter, 1998)
10–11 years	■ May use organizational strategies when instructed to remember information without prompting (Chance & Fischman, 1987) ■ Begin using rehearsal strategies, such as grouping items together or repeating them in a certain sequence
12 years	■ Use more spontaneous elaboration and strategies independently

Even by age 3, a child should be able to do this correctly if he has heard and taken in the information. If your child cannot do this, you might have his hearing checked by the pediatrician or explore the possibility of some auditory processing problems via a psychologist or audiologist. Secondly, attention is a prerequisite for memory, so this is another area to analyze. When an important request is made, having eye contact with your child is one step you can take to try to ensure proper attention is there. If your child is a daydreamer, inattention will be harder to detect. Sometimes knowing they will be asked to repeat directions encourages children to pay better attention. Thirdly, try to determine if failure to complete the task is behavioral as opposed to a working memory issue. As an intuitive parent, you probably have a pretty good idea if your child just doesn't want to be bothered by fulfilling your request or if he can't keep the request in memory long enough to complete it. If it is behavioral, then your approach will need to address the issue through consequences and positive reinforcement.

It is very important to provide a stimulating environment with access to opportunities to experience new things as a way of improving your child's memory.

If you have determined that your child likely has difficulties with working memory, it is important to implement scaffolding supports as previously discussed in Chapter 2.

Helping the 4- to 5-Year-Old Child

Children in this age group are very prompt dependent for many tasks, including those that require working memory. We know that young children don't have the capacity or experience to enable them to operate without structure and assistance. If your child has a chore list, it is likely a visual list that is easily followed. Some children even need a visual sequence for tasks, such as brushing teeth or getting dressed, because they can't keep all of the steps in memory. To make the chart, you can use pictures from the computer to represent the chores. Some parents like to photograph their child performing the different parts of the task.

To help build your young child's working memory, give your child lots of practice with using memory skills. Some parents find it easier to go ahead and do things for their children rather than instructing and asking them to do things for themselves. We don't advocate this because by giving your young child short directions to follow, you are providing valuable practice in using working memory skills. When she can successfully complete a one-step direction, add two steps to the request, such as "Go get your hairbrush and your shoes." Success in these kinds of activities could be the beginning of motivation, so try to praise and appreciate small accomplishments.

Always make sure you have eye contact with her before giving a direction she is to remember and follow. Timing and situation are important, so try to minimize the competing distractions when giving a direction. You want to optimize the child's chances for remembering, so try to avoid giving information in noisy, chaotic environments or while she is looking at a screen. If the direction is really important, stress that to the child. If you sense that she is confused, ask her to repeat the direction to ensure she has understood what you are asking.

Keep directions simple and avoid wordiness. It is important to deliver just enough information to get the job done and not too much that working memory will be overloaded. For more than one direction, offer a recap. For example, when Lana was given a two-step direction, her mother said as a summary of the two tasks, "Remember, Lana, I want you to get two things—your socks and your shorts." You might even have her hold up two fingers as a reminder of how many items she should bring back.

Working memory for a young child is not just following simple directions but also involves recalling similar situations and outcomes, thinking of consequences, and considering potential rewards. It stands to reason that the ability to keep these kinds of information in memory aids the child in making good choices. It is important to guide your child in recalling similar events and applying that information to a current situation. Even stories you have read to him that involved similar events can be helpful in helping him learn to assess events and relate them to previous experiences.

Teaching 6- to 12-Year-Olds to Maximize their Working Memory

As your child matures, you will expect her to become more independent, think for herself, and require fewer prompts and reminders from you. She will be expected to keep more and more information in working memory, like her schedule and responsibilities for the day, materials and supplies needed, and commitments made to other people.

Remembering Activities and Materials or Equipment

Many children participate in at least one sport or activity. How many times have you arrived at a sports practice to find you child has forgotten part of his equipment? Again, it is tempting to remember all of the items yourself, but you are not helping your child develop working memory. Brainstorm ways with him that he can remember the necessary pieces of equipment. Bryan came up with the idea of visualizing himself before his baseball practices—starting at his head and thinking of his helmet, then his eyes and remembering sunglasses, next his face and remembering sunscreen, etc. Stephanie chose to look at a poster of a basketball player on her wall to jog her memory about what she needed to take to practice. Jonathan was packing for a school trip and tried to visualize what he would need for each day. As children get older, they should be developing some awareness about how their memory works and what they can do to help themselves—with your continued support and guidance, of course. Encourage them to come up with their own strategies and share ideas that work for you. We can't stress enough that good organizational strategies can significantly lessen the load on working memory.

Following Through on Chores

In our practices, we find that chores are almost always a sore subject. It is very difficult to sort out whether the chores are not done because your child forgot or whether that is just a convenient excuse. Even though seeing that chores are completed is a source of much friction between parent and child, it is an important part of your child's training and move toward independence—your ultimate goal. In today's busy households, it is important for everyone to pull his or her weight. If significant prompting is needed to ensure chores are done, a chart will provide a visual reminder. Sit down with your child and develop a list of chores and when they need to be completed. As with most of us, rewards are reinforcing, so they should also be part of your discussion. Help your child use the computer to come up with a chart listing the chores to be done, as well as consequences and rewards. Ensuring that the chart is followed will be an extra duty for you but could be well worth it in the long run.

Financial expert Dave Ramsey recommends not paying your child a flat fee for completing all of his or her chores but rather paying your child a commission for each chore. If your son completes each of his weekly chores, he earns a commission for each chore but if he forgets or does not follow through, then no money is earned for that chore. Thus, kids learn responsibility and the value of work from an early age. Simply put, if they don't work, they don't get paid. Even though chores can be a hassle, your child will learn valuable lessons related to memory, follow-through, and how to get work done even if it's not fun.

More Memory Strategies

Mnemonic strategies are ways of helping people use lists, first letters of words, rhymes, music, images, spelling, or connections to remember longer lists or strings of information. All of us have probably used mnemonic strategies in school or in our personal life to help us recall specific information. Some types of mnemonics are as follows:

- *Music mnemonics*: songs like the "Days of the Week" song preschoolers sing
- *Name mnemonics*: one of the oldest is ROY G. BIV to recall the colors in the rainbow: Red, Orange, Yellow, Green, Blue, Indigo, and Violet
- *Rhyme mnemonics*: like one of the spelling rules, "i " before "e" except after "c."
- *Image mnemonics*: use of a picture or visual image to help remember something, like a person's name
- *Connection mnemonics*: information that is connected to something already known; for example, remembering that "Horizontal" goes across like the center line of the "H" and "Vertical" is the opposite.
- *Spelling mnemonics*: relating the letters in a word to a saying, like GEOGRAPHY: George Ellis' Old Grandma Rode a Pig Home Yesterday (Congos, 2006).

Organization strategies—another efficient way to foster working memory—include putting things in lists, organizing information into categories, outlining, or making notecards.

Books for Children

Children enjoy being read to and these books are ones you can read to and with your child to help your child learn about strengthening memory. Follow the framework of: (a) read the book ahead of time to make sure it's appropriate; (b) read to or with your child and pause to discuss the book's ideas; (c) discuss how the book's character used the skill or solved a problem; and (d) discuss how the ideas can help in your family or at school. The books below are available online or in major bookstores.

- o *I Am Really, Really Concentrating* (Charlie and Lola) by Lauren Child, for ages 3–5
- o *I Just Forgot* (A Little Critter Book) by Mercer Mayer, for ages 3–7
- o *Ollie Forgot* by Tedd Arnold, for ages 5 and up

At School

Working memory issues in school become more apparent as the child progresses through the grades. In preschool and kindergarten, the teacher orally and with gestures prompts children in their daily tasks and often uses visual reminders as well. In kindergarten and in most first grades, children still have alphabet and number strips on their desks in case they forget how a letter is formed. They may also require a number and alphabet strip attached to their desk or included in their notebook after first grade until they are proficient at recalling how to write letters and numbers. Children with these difficulties have weakness with the "visual-spatial sketchpad," which holds and uses visual and spatial material (Baddeley, 1986). Visual-spatial skills are very developmental in nature and occur along a continuum at various times for different children. It is important to remember that reversals of letters and numbers can be developmental until the age of 8. If they persist after that time and impact the child's school performance, he could have a learning disability and should be tested either through the school or privately by a school or clinical psychologist.

Consider your child. Read the examples below of how executive functioning difficulties in working memory appear in school. Do any apply to your child?

- o Can't remember the teacher's directions to get started on a task
- o Can't keep times tables in memory while solving a math word problem involving multiplication
- o Doesn't remember details of what he has just read

○ Isn't allowed to go on a field trip because she forgot to return the permission slip

○ Gets a low grade on his writing assignment because he forgot to use capitalization and punctuation

○ Performs poorly on tests because she doesn't recall information

○ Is often chosen last for games because he has trouble keeping track of the directions

Some young children do have difficulty learning and following the daily classroom schedule and may benefit from scaffolded support using a picture schedule taped to their desk coupled with significant prompting and assistance from a teacher or adult until the schedule is mastered. As they get older, the scaffolded prompts fade and children are expected to become more independent.

Tracy is 5-year-old girl who is known for her pretty face and cute expressions. She goes to school on time but often forgets her backpack, lunch bag, and water bottle, despite reminders from her mother. When she arrives at school, she has trouble remembering the morning routine and needs prompting from her teacher. When Tracy leaves the class for lunchtime, she forgets to grab her lunch and has to go back to the class to retrieve it. When it's time to go home, she forgets which bus she rides.

In addition to verbal prompts, Tracy needs visual reminders to help her focus on and remember important things in her daily routine. Her mother and Tracy find an area by the door where Tracy can place her backpack as soon as she has finished any homework she may have. Then her mother places a small picture right by the door showing each item Tracy needs to leave with on school days. Tracy is required to stop, put her finger on each picture, and check to make sure she has that item. At school, her teacher continues prompting but also made a laminated visual schedule that Tracy keeps on her desk and paired her with a positive role model. As an added incentive to remember her lunchbox when leaving the classroom for lunch, Tracy is allowed to sit with a friend if she remembers the lunchbox without a reminder. At the end of the day, she is paired with a classmate who rides the same bus. Also, in an effort to make her more independent, she has a large sticker on her backpack with the bus number on it so she can look at it before boarding the bus. Teacher supervisors at the bus area are alerted to Tracy's difficulties and know to double check to ensure she gets on the correct bus. As Tracy demonstrates better working memory skills, the scaffolding will slowly be removed.

Middle school brings a heavier load on working memory as students have more classes, teachers, and materials. Many middle schoolers with working memory difficulties are completely bamboozled by the increased load of details to remember. It is helpful if your child's middle school eases her in to the challenges of keeping up with so many moving parts and continues to provide reminders and prompts until she develops a routine, which takes some of the load off of her working memory. Children with working memory difficulties often also suffer from poor organizational skills, which only compound their problems in middle school. Scheduling extra time at the beginning of their middle school year to ensure they have some organized approach to managing their school day can yield big benefits in the long run. It is important to review their schedule; make sure they have an organized procedure for dealing with notes, classwork, and homework; and have a method of remembering and keeping track of assignments.

Traditionally, school has been considered to be very language-based, with much information delivered to children orally. Children with delays in either expressive or receptive language are at a distinct disadvantage in taking in, processing, and understanding material, which would understandably affect their working memory. Additionally, children who process information slowly may have difficulty. Once oral information is provided, there is frequently no way to check or reference what was said. That information is gone. Some teachers will allow students to audio-record class discussions. If your child has a disability, such as ADHD or a learning disability, a 504 plan or IEP are support plans that detail accommodations and support if your child meets eligibility criteria. A more detailed discussion of these plans can be found in our previous books, *Raising Boys With ADHD* and *Raising Girls With ADHD*.

Working Memory Problems in Specific Academic Areas

Math. Young children often have difficulty remembering what a specific number looks like when initially learning to write numbers. They should have access to a number line placed on their desk as long as necessary. Using their sense of touch is often helpful in assisting their recall, like writing numbers in sand or writing them very large on a sidewalk with chalk and then walking over the number and repeating it to themselves while walking. Counting multiple items can also be confusing because they may forget which items they have already counted. Try to help them learn to start at the same place on the left side and count out loud slowly to themselves while pointing with their finger.

As children get older, keeping numbers in mind while performing mathematical calculations can be a significant problem. Again, converting some of that information into visuals can be helpful. Memorizing math facts is often difficult and time consuming. Repeated practice with flash cards and reinforcement on the computer can be helpful.

Reading. The early stages of reading can be impacted by weak working memory because the child is not able to keep the visual of the letter in memory while attaching a name or sound to it. This slows down the letter and sound identification process significantly if the child has to search his memory for the name of the letter rather than having it be an automatic, fluid process. Sometimes the issue is related to the visual-spatial sketchpad where visual images are held in memory. Other times, it is related to fluency or how fast the eye converts images, processes them, and provides output. It can also be related to attention. If a child does not focus on a letter long enough to process and retain it, clearly it can't go into his memory bank. Provide the child with an alphabet strip and lots of practice with letter identification.

Reading skills are developmental in nature and don't develop at the same time for all children. However, if your child is having significant difficulty with letter identification and letter sound associations, he or she could have a learning disability. Speak with your child's school or have a private evaluation done by a psychologist if you are concerned. With so many problems, early intervention is a key. Systematic phonics instruction, like the Wilson Reading System or Orton-Gillingham based multisensory reading instruction, is helpful for children with significant delays and learning disabilities, like dyslexia.

As the reading process progresses, attempts to decode words can be significantly hampered when the child can't remember the initial sounds decoded in order to blend them with the medial and ending sounds. Frustration with this process often results in children "ball parking" words or pronouncing them based only on their first letter rather than going through the laborious process of decoding them sound-by-sound. Obviously misreading one or two words in a passage can change the whole meaning. It is important to help the child understand the importance each syllable plays in a word and try to build sight word vocabulary, while strengthening decoding skills through intensive practice. Remember this can be a frustrating process for your child, so finding interesting ways to reinforce skills, such as through apps or programs on the Internet or computer, is important.

Fluency is another important skill to develop and is strongly related to comprehension. If reading is not fluid and automatic, students will be focused on decoding words and unable to concentrate on what they are reading. Practice for fluency involves reading the passages at their grade level aloud with few mistakes on a daily basis until they become fluent. Oftentimes, the same passages are read 3 or 4 times to a parent, tutor, or older sibling. They can also be read into an audio recorder and played back.

As reading skills progress, children with working memory difficulties often have poor reading comprehension because they are not able to hold details in memory long enough to get the gist or main idea of the passage they are reading. Much of their working memory capacity is used up trying to decode words rather than developing a broad understanding of what they are reading. Before beginning to read, students should:

o try to make sure they are in an environment conducive to focusing on the content;

o preview the information to orient themselves to what they will be reading about and access any prior knowledge they may have about the topic;

- o become an active reader, try to place themselves in the story, question what they are reading, predict outcomes, etc.;
- o underline key words and/or use a story map or some sort of organizational chart to keep track of important details;
- o pose questions to themselves as they are reading and try to be aware when they are not understanding what they are reading;
- o summarize to themselves or in writing what they have read; and
- o in later childhood, employ analytical thought to what has been read and "read between the lines"—making inferences from the text.

Writing. The process of getting our thoughts down on paper is very complex, involving heavy requirements on working memory. To communicate effectively, the student has to think creatively and organize ideas while keeping grammar and spelling in mind. Often, this is an overload for students with weak working memory.

For younger children with difficulties recalling how to form letters and words, the process can be quite laborious. As noted previously, children with difficulty with letter and number formation and identification will need an alphabet and number strip on their desks. It is important for these young students to develop any story ideas they have, so allowing them to dictate stories to an adult encourages their creativity while alleviating some of the frustration. Inventive spelling is encouraged to motivate children to put their stories in writing until their spelling skills are more developed.

Older students with working memory difficulties benefit from using a monitoring strategy for editing their papers. One such method is COPS, where the student would go back and check his composition for:

- o **C**apitalization;
- o **O**verall appearance: margins, complete sentences, and paragraph indentation;
- o **P**unctuation: internal punctuation, like commas, as well as end punctuation; and
- o **S**pelling.

A detailed discussion of writing intervention is included in *Executive Function in the Classroom: Practical Strategies for Improving Performance and Enhancing Skills for All Students* by Christopher Kaufman, licensed psychologist.

Social Difficulties Related to Working Memory

Social difficulties often arise in children with working memory deficits because they are not effective in recalling consequences of similar past actions to guide their current behavior. A preschool child may not recall being put in a brief timeout for hitting his brother in the head. An older child may not remember losing a friend because he insisted on having his way. Social experiences are very complex with many different skills coming together to form an interaction, so it is difficult to sort out what has caused the difficulties. Impulsivity often plays a role in young children's social problems because they are not able to slow down long enough to consider consequences, but if poor working memory causes failure to remember the past events, your child is even more at risk for social problems. Photographs have been shown to improve children's recall of events. If you have a picture from a birthday party or outing where a situation occurred, you might use that visual in helping the child recall the setting and then go on to discuss events that occurred and brainstorm reactions that might have resulted in better outcomes.

Social difficulties often arise in children with working memory deficits because they are not effective in recalling consequences of similar past actions to guide their current behavior.

Another area where poor working memory causes social difficulties is in remembering names, social greetings, and showing appreciation for gifts or nice gestures. Although children may love a gift they have received from a grandparent, the appreciation for that present may not stay in their working memory

Suggestions for the Teacher

Deficits in executive functioning, like an inefficient working memory, can significantly impact children in the classroom. We wanted to offer some suggestions that might help improve classroom functioning.

o Make sure the child has the foundation for what you are teaching. If the foundation is not in place, the child will have difficulty grasping and retaining concepts that build on that base. Sometimes parents are open to providing private tutoring or reinforcing skills at home, especially if deficits are pinpointed.

o Try not to show frustration or surprise with the student's lack of memory. As frustrated as you might be that your student has lost the information you tried so hard to effectively teach yesterday, imagine how difficult this is for the child.

o Make lessons as interesting and interactive as possible. Ensuring that a child is paying attention is the first step to helping him or her remember information. Sometimes it helps to have a special signal that only you and the child know, such as a tap on the shoulder, to alert the child that important information that needs to be remembered is coming, so he needs to focus.

o Hands-on and experiential learning can foster attention and retention. If a child's attention and interest have been captured, he or she is more likely to remember material.

o Use visuals to accompany auditory information, providing two ways for the information to enter memory.

o Try to help the child associate what is being taught with something he already knows. If he can make that association, it will be much easier to pull out information from long-term storage.

Suggestions for the Teacher, continued

o   Frequently children with memory problems also have difficulty with organization. Help them see how the skill you are teaching fits in a structure or bigger picture.

o   Once a child has mastered a concept, having him or her teach that concept to another child has been shown to improve retention.

o   Frequent repetition and review are necessary. "Use it or lose it" applies to all learning.

o   Use the computer to reinforce skills and provide review.

o   Provide an outline listing steps for multistep problems, such as steps in regrouping double-digit subtraction problems.

o   Implement a way to track and measure small learning gains so the child can see that the effort he puts in pays off. For any of us, continually mustering up the effort to work hard at something that we will likely not be successful at is difficult.

o   Use flashcards and other reminders to reinforce and practice skills.

o   Have the student use checklists to make sure steps have not been forgotten, such as in writing a composition or completing multistep math problems.

long enough for them to issue a thank you unless they have practiced and rehearsed what they will say with a parent. Helping them learn to express appreciation right away enhances the chances that they will remember to do it.

In conversation, some children with poor working memory interrupt and interject with their own input before waiting for the other person to finish speaking because they are afraid they will forget what they want to say. Helping them focus on the speaker and actively listen while trying to keep their thought in their "mind's eye" is important.

In the Community

It is not surprising that working memory deficits would impact your child in the community as well as in other areas of his life. Some of these difficulties include:

- Failing to remember which items he was supposed to get when you sent him in to the grocery store
- Not being allowed to complete a scout project because he forgot all of the materials he was supposed to bring
- Forgetting to attend a birthday party that had only a verbal invitation
- Isn't a successful conversationalist because he can't keep information in memory during a conversation and forgets what he wants to say

Your goal is for your child to have positive experiences in the community despite his or her working memory difficulties. If these deficits impact your child in extracurricular activities, like dance or karate lesson or sports teams, it will be important to help the teacher or coach know what strategies will be effective for your child. For example, keeping directions succinct and providing written handouts of any lengthy information would be helpful. Encourage your child to ask questions when information is forgotten or unclear. After practice or the lesson, try to review important information with your child as soon as possible before it vanishes from working memory. Remember, it will be important for you to advocate for your child until he is able to take on that job for himself.

Leveraging Strengths

By observation, help your child determine how he or she remembers information best. Some children have strengths in either visual or auditory memory, some benefit from a combination of the two, and some even find using rhythm helps them remember. Making a rap or song out of steps in a process makes remembering easier and more interesting for some. Many of us remember the "Clean Up, Clean Up" song from preschool and kindergarten days or the *Grammar Rock* show.

By observation, help your child determine how he or she remembers information best. Some children have strengths in either visual or auditory memory, some benefit from a combination of the two and some even find using rhythm helps them remember.

If you or your child is a visual learner, jotting down information as it is spoken is helpful. It focuses attention and provides a reminder long after the auditory direction or information has disappeared. Many adults and older children type information into a notes section on a phone or other device. If your child is an auditory learner, he might repeat information several times to himself to cement it in memory until it is needed to complete a task.

If your child has good organizational skills, she can set up the environment to reduce the load on working memory. Consistently following routines becomes habitual and takes working memory out of the equation as so many actions become automatic. This is especially helpful if she has specific places to keep items such as her backpack or cell phone chargers, so she does not have to remember where she left them.

If your child has good relationships with his classmates, he can often receive a hand from other students. Having the phone numbers of several students he can contact if he forgets needed information is often helpful. If a student has difficulty getting information down on paper, he can often check with other students or the teacher to ensure he has recorded assignments or information correctly. Teachers will often check individual student agendas for accuracy if asked.

Leveraging Technology

You can help your child learn to use technology to lessen the load on working memory and provide much needed prompts. Below are suggested strategies for using technology.

- o Use automatic reminders on a phone or device if available.
- o Use the mini-me recording device (similar to the chip in greeting cards) to record a short 10-second message of important school materials to bring home or routine tasks to complete before bedtime. You could place one in the bathroom and have your child play it to hear "brush teeth, wash face, floss."
- o Use an electronic calendar to keep track of important events.
- o Incorporate e-mail or text reminders into your calendars.
- o Use apps to make flashcards for study. Many apps allow the user to track progress over time.
- o Use Inspiration or Kidspiration or other software to help with organizing writing.
- o Use Evernote for electronic note taking or Notes on the phone for keeping track of information.
- o Use text-to-speech software.
- o Try out web-based programs for strengthening memory, such as Cogmed or Lumosity.

Lumosity (http://www.lumosity.com) is available online and offers some free memory games, but for a fee, subscribers are provided with more programs as well as some progress monitoring tools. Cogmed (http://www.cogmed.com) is also done online with support and assistance from a coach who monitors progress and checks in weekly. It is fee-based, has a set number of sessions, and allows for use of the program after the coach-monitored sessions are completed. Both programs have some independent research supporting their effectiveness.

Next Steps

After reading this chapter, take a minute for the following exercise.

An idea I can put into action is . . .

_____

_____

_____

_____

_____

_____

_____

_____

_____

_____

_____

_____

_____

_____

_____

_____

_____

_____

CHAPTER 5

Shifting, Being Flexible, and Regulating Emotion

"I can't change the direction of the wind, but I can adjust my sails to always reach my destination."—Jimmy Dean

Self-Reflection Survey

1. The ability to shift activities and thoughts, as well as be flexible, makes it much easier to be resilient in the face of difficulty.
   a. true   b. false

2. A child's temperament:
   a. has an innate component
   b. can't be changed
   c. influences emotional regulation
   d. is affected by circumstances and environmental conditions
   e. all but one of the above

3. My child's difficulty with flexibility and emotional control occurs mostly at:
   a. home
   b. school
   c. playground
   d. team sports

4. My child has some strategies to use when he feels overwhelmed by a situation:
   a. true
   b. false

Answers: 1. a, 2. e (all except b)

Is It a Problem With Shifting, Being Flexible, and/or Regulating Emotion?

If the behaviors listed below describe your child, then you are in the right area:
- Gets upset when he can't be first in line
- Tattles often when other children are not following rules
- Freaks out if plans change suddenly
- Is very finicky about food and will only eat foods prepared a certain way
- Cries if he misses a test item or can't figure out how to do a problem
- Wants to transition between activities on his own schedule
- Becomes sad or angry easily and has trouble shaking these feelings
- Thinks in concrete "black" and "white" terms with no room for "gray"

We live in a fast-paced world with change occurring almost daily. Being resilient and able to adjust to change will be even more critical as your child becomes a young adult. Temperament plays a big role in flexibility. We all know people who seem to be extremely rigid by nature and others who "go with the flow" no matter where it takes them. However, resiliency is something you can foster in your children by exposing them to change and giving them tools to cope with it. We are not suggesting you try to change your child's personality, simply help her learn to cope with change so it will not be so stressful for her. If your child tends to like routines or be on the rigid side, you will have to work harder at it, but you can improve her ability to maintain her composure when plans have to be changed. We have included self-regulation in this chapter because emotional outbursts often accompany inflexibility—whether it is from the inability to share a toy or to accept that a situation is not going to unfold as the child had expected.

What Does Shifting and Being Flexible Entail?

Shifting and being flexible refer to the ability to change how you think about things and to accept changes when what you are presented with is *not* what you had expected. Some people are much more comfortable with routine and seem to have difficulty shifting their thought patterns and thinking about alternative solutions. They see the world in a black-and-white perspective with little room for ambiguity. The causes for this kind of rigidity are many—genes, temperament, and environmental and cultural factors all play significant roles. Difficulty with flexibility and shifting thought are much more apparent in some disorders, like autism spectrum disorder or conduct disorder, than others.

We often refer to children who can shift their thinking and be flexible as being resilient. This means that the children can bounce back

> *Shifting and being flexible refer to the ability to change how you think about things and to accept changes when what you are presented with is not what you had expected.*

from disappointments, handle stress, generate solutions to problems, and remain positive. Children who are resilient generally have good self-esteem and are able to establish a network of friends and supportive people. They often take their cues from parents and important adults in their lives about how to approach problems and make the best of difficult situations. Their coping skills develop over time. Remember, as your children are growing up, they are continually watching you for cues on how to handle stressful situations. If you are intolerant of others, they will likely be also. If you show your frustration when plans don't work out, your children may well do the same.

What Is Emotional Control?

Emotional control refers to the ability to maintain command of your outward expression of emotions as well as your negative inner feelings, like anxiety, guilt, frustration, and disappointment. If you have emotional control, you do not let yourself get mired down in unpleasant emotions but can redirect your thoughts to more positive, productive ones. Expectations for the degree of emotional control vary significantly with age. We expect much more from a 10-year-old than a 4-year-old.

Emotional control refers to the ability to maintain command of your outward expression of emotions as well as your negative inner feelings, like anxiety, guilt, frustration, and disappointment.

As with all executive functions, emotional control often depends on the situation. Many of our clients with ADHD are able to demonstrate emotional control at school, but lose some of that ability in the home. That is understandable because they are more comfortable at home and feel safer, it is much less structured, and it is a more private setting where children often feel they can let their guard down. Some children, especially those who are impulsive, feel they have "used up" all of their emotional control by the time they get home and have few reserves left. It is still important to have boundaries for behavior and definite limits on the types of outbursts you will tolerate for your child's well-being, as well as your own.

As we have noted, emotional control is not just about controlling outbursts and temper tantrums. It is also about managing other negative emotions, like worry, anxiety, or sadness. Just as children with executive functioning problems might have trouble shifting their thinking in other areas, they might also have that same difficulty letting go of negative emotions. Once they develop anxiety about a situation, they might stay in that frame of mind much longer than is healthy. Frequently children with executive function problems have difficulty with social and school success, so their self-esteem and their confidence in their ability to take charge and change things suffer too. Problems for children with weakened executive functioning can be compounded by poor sustained attention that would prevent them from staying focused on a situation long enough to completely understand what is going on, or weak working memory that would not allow them to recall similar previous events and their outcomes. It becomes obvious why these children would need support to handle and process what is going on around them.

University of South Florida researchers, in collaboration with the Parent Advisory Coalition for Educational Rights, have developed a series of information sheets entitled "Making Life Easier." They are written for parents to help with understanding the difficulties young children have with flexibility and regulating their emotions. Four of these information sheets are included in the Appendix at the back of this book. They are entitled, "Going to the Doctor/Dentist," "Bedtime and Naptime," "Running Errands," and "Holiday Strategies" (Buschbacher, 2010). They provide specific steps for developing routines for daily events like bedtime and preparing your child for events that are outside of his or her daily routines, like doing errands, celebrating holidays, and going to medical appointments.

Developmental Context

Table 3 gives some general developmental guidelines of what to expect at different ages as resiliency and behavioral control develop.

Shifting and Being Flexible

General Strategies

Develop a consistent, predictable daily routine with a visual schedule if needed. This does not need to be a rigid, detailed schedule but enough structure so children know the important things in their lives—mealtimes, bedtime, etc.—have some predictability.

Try not to allow your child to develop habits that will make life difficult for him or her. Some children are very routine oriented and need that sameness to help them handle their anxiety. This is especially true of children on the autism spectrum. As a parent, you understand how much sameness your child requires in order to function effectively. Honoring that will certainly make your life go smoother. However, you should always be trying to modify habits that are so highly specific that they are bound to cause disappointment over time. For example, if your child insists on the same cereal for breakfast, try to help him think of some other choices that would be acceptable. When he breaks his routine and selects an alternative choice for breakfast, reinforce and praise that flexibility. Although structure at home is necessary, especially for the daily schedule, your life will be easier the more flexible your child can become about other aspects of his day.

Prepare them for changes. Provide advance warnings when transitions are coming. For example, give a 5-minute warning and then a 1-minute warning before children are expected to change activities. If taking a trip, show them pictures of the destination and talk with them about travel plans.

Help them develop strategies for handling change when they are not prepared for it. Children who can seek out a supportive adult or peer are much more successful in handling an unexpected event.

Table 3. Guidelines for Resiliency and
Behavioral Control Development

2–5 years	■ Can shift actions based on changing rules (e.g. run on the playground but not inside) ■ Begins to understand turn-taking ■ Emerging understanding of time ■ Emotions can still be very intense ■ Difficulty separating "real" from "imaginary" ■ May develop fears
3 years	■ "Can direct and re-direct their attention to make deliberate choices," mental flexibility (Center on the Developing Child, 2011, p. 4).
5 years	■ Can play cooperatively with several children
6–9 years	■ Self-control continues to improve ■ Internal thinking or self-talk develops ■ Becomes better able to control negative feelings ■ Develops awareness of consequences of their actions ■ Begins to understand difference between "needs" and "wants" ■ More sophisticated understanding of time ■ Still egocentric but beginning to understand perspectives of others ■ Peer competition in sports and the classroom comes to the forefront
10–12 years	■ Becomes more flexible according to changing rules (Can use calculator on homework, not on classwork, and only on some standardized tests) ■ Better able to separate actions and feelings and control negative feelings (Teeter, 1998) ■ Able to take more responsibility for their actions ■ Wants independence but still needs guidance ■ Importance of peer acceptance increasing

As they become older, children can use internal dialogue to process change and assure themselves that it will be okay and figure out ways to handle it.

Point out their flexibility when you observe it. If we want our children to value and recognize flexibility, then we have to praise them and call attention to it when they are. For example, compliment your child for allowing his or her brother or sister to go first.

Implement changes that can be fun. Make up games that could be a variation of a familiar game like Red Rover. Change characters in stories, such as letting Goldilocks take on a different and possibly a silly role. Trying foods from another culture or taking food on a picnic at a park as opposed to eating inside can demonstrate that change can be fun.

Regulating Emotions

General Strategies

Be a role model. As difficult as it is, try to exhibit emotional control and civil discourse in front of your children. They take their cues from you. Studies on bullying show that children who bully often learn their disrespectful language and behavior from parents. You will set the emotional tone in your home and want your children to be comfortable discussing their thoughts and feelings in an atmosphere of respect.

Read stories aloud to your children and discuss how various characters handled their feelings. Books provide a concrete way for students to relate to a character's experiences.

Prepare to use meaningful rewards and have consistent consequences for willful misbehavior. Children who have difficulty with regulating emotions often benefit from rewards that are truly motivating to them as an additional incentive to try to exhibit that control. Some people see that as rewarding them for doing a behavior they should be doing anyway, but we have to keep in mind that there is a neurological component to executive functioning difficulties. If you characterize your child as having a "short fuse," then it may be significantly more difficult for him to control his emotions than another child. If your child is prone to anxiety and worry, then he will require assistance in learning how to handle those feelings and motivation to use the strategies you suggest. That is where the meaningful rewards come in—to add that extra motivation to do something that doesn't come naturally and requires mental energy.

When an outburst occurs, try to do a skill autopsy on the situation—determining what caused it and any intervening factors that encouraged or prolonged it. Obviously, if the outburst was related to fear or anxiety, you would not have consequences. However, if the behavior resulted from uncontrolled anger and involved physical aggression or abusive language, you would have to implement consequences. Time out without stimulation (adjusted for age) or losing a privilege could be consequences. If the same behavior occurs repeatedly, then it will be important to sit down and come up with alternative ways of handling the anger or frustration and agree upon consequences if the behavior does occur. As difficult as it is, you must remember to stick to the plan. When Mary Anne's children were younger, she would always think, "If I don't follow through with what I said, it will be twice as hard the next time." Consistency cannot be overestimated. Additionally, it is important for rewards or consequences to be delivered as close to the behavior as possible for it to be meaningful.

In the Home

Helping the 4- to 5-Year-Old Child

As you know, preschoolers are complex little people. So many of their behaviors are influenced by their physical state—whether they are tired, bored, hungry, or overstimulated. Trying to plan your youngster's day so those factors don't come in to play will make your life much easier. Your child's facility with language will also be a big factor in his ability to manage change and behavior. If your child can articulate what is making him angry or anxious, then he will be more likely to handle it without a big scene. Try to enlarge your child's vocabulary of "feeling" words. Talk about situations when you are angry or frustrated because your day is interrupted by something aggravating and what you did about it. Help your child see how you talk it out and handle it. Young children are always watching and modeling their parents.

When unexpected changes occur, help the child understand what will happen and how that is different from what he expected. For younger children, try to make it as visual as you can. If possible, help him relate the change to something he has already experienced that didn't turn out badly. If a preferred activity has to be canceled, then help your child understand why and let him help you reschedule it if possible. Writing the rescheduled activity on a simple calendar will make it seem more real to the child. Remember that at this age, they have a limited concept of time.

Try to identify warning signs that he is beginning to lose control and try to intervene at that point by disrupting his thought pattern by offering a distraction, prompting him to step away from the situation, or using a strategy like stopping and thinking before acting. Use your own knowledge of your child's temperament. Some children need their own space to calm down; others need the comforting support of an adult or an item of attachment, such as a stuffed animal.

Preventing tantrums when the schedule changes unexpectedly. As we have noted, many children become very dependent on things unfolding exactly as they expect. Some children are very rigid in their thought patterns, find a comfort level in routines, or are just insistent on having their own way. If your child is insistent on routines, talk with him about changes ahead of time if possible. Help him process the change, understand how it will happen, and why the change is necessary. If an activity is cancelled, planning a replacement activity can be a good distraction. If plans change because someone is sick, then try to involve your child in doing something for that person. Your ultimate goal will be to try to help the child figure out ways to recover from the disappointment.

When he can't have his way. Young children are very egocentric and have a very hard time considering any other perspective but their own. Some children are very strong-willed and determined to have things their way. When power struggles erupt, it is important to intervene before the situation escalates if you are sure the child cannot return to equilibrium without help. If the child has not escalated to the point where you cannot reason with him, then let him know concisely why he can't have his way. Sometimes you can help the child reason through the situation and consider other choices. If it is an altercation with another child over who was the winner, then remind him of the rules of fair play and that no one can be the winner all of the time. If it is a desire to stay with a current activity and not move on to the next, then remind him of the schedule and show him a visual schedule if available. If it is anger over not being allowed a toy at the store, then explain clearly that you cannot buy it at this time. If he has something similar, then remind him of that and how much he enjoys playing with it. If he progresses to a tantrum, then let him know you are leaving the store as soon as you can. Whatever you do, do not allow your child to get what he wants by throwing a tantrum—you will only be reinforcing it.

During lunchtime, Jill, a preschooler, enjoys showing her friends her princess lunchbox and what is inside of it. Suddenly, she sees that a classmate has gummy bears as a treat. Jill begins to cry because she does not have any. Jill's teacher comforts her by showing her all of the other delicious foods that she does have and suggesting that she let her mommy know that she would like gummy bears in her lunch. After Jill's teacher has helped her cope with this dilemma, Jill is able to continue to enjoy her lunch.

Dealing With 6- to 12-Year-Olds

Having a tantrum when frustrated. Some children with inflexible behavior are very perfectionistic. They have a very hard time if they can't solve a homework problem successfully or if something they are doing at home doesn't turn out perfectly. Sometimes their disappointment is so intense that they lose behavioral control and stomp, scream, or cry like a much younger child. You can be sure that when her frustration has reached this level, her "thinking" brain has probably shut down. At this point, it is important for the child to go to a quiet place to calm down and get herself together before there can be any discussion about what happened. As soon as she is calm and rational, help her step back and look at the behavior that occurred and generate some alternative behaviors that would have resulted in much better outcomes.

Becoming upset when others do not follow rules. Children who have a very rigid view of the world often get perturbed when others do not follow the rules. A rigid child may try to continually tattle on siblings or chastise them if she does not feel they are following the rules. It is important to help her understand that the adult in the home is the one in charge of enforcing the rules, and rules are guidelines that can be influenced by extenuating circumstances.

More Strategies to Encourage Resilience and Emotional Stability in Older Children

To help children improve cognitive flexibility and emotional control:

o   Let them help you decide how to change up rules for a favorite game to make it more fun.

o   Play games like *Clue* where the situations change each game for the characters.

o   Help them become better at reading body language so they can tell when they have annoyed or offended someone.

o   Explore different calming or mindfulness techniques with them, such as deep breathing, exercise, yoga, listening to music or meditating, until they find and use something that works for them.

o   Nurture their relationships with family members and friends.

o   Help them develop a confidence in their ability to solve problems with the support of adults.

o   Role-play situations with your child. Handling emotionally charged situations can be very tough for any of us, but especially for children, so they can benefit from practice. Take turns with your child playing different people in scenarios where conflict, sadness, or anxiety occurs. Afterward, discuss different situations and how they will serve the character in the long run.

Books for Children

Children enjoy being read to and these are books you can read to and with your child. Follow the framework outlined in previous chapters, which included: (a) read the book ahead of time to make sure it's appropriate; (b) read to or with your child and pause to discuss the book's ideas; (c) discuss how the book's character used the skill or solved a problem; and (d) discuss how the ideas can help in your family or at school.

- o *No, no, NO!* by Marie-Isabelle Callier, for ages 4–6
- o *Chillax!: How Ernie Learns to Chill Out, Relax, and Take Charge of His Anger* by Marcella Marino Craver, for ages 10–12
- o *Josh's Smiley Faces: A Story About Anger* by Gina Ditta-Donahue, for ages 4 and up
- o *What to Do When Your Temper Flares: A Kid's Guide to Overcoming Problems With Anger* by Dawn Huebner, for ages 8 and up
- o *What to Do When It's Not Fair: A Kid's Guide to Handling Envy and Jealousy* by Jacqueline Toner and Claire Freeland, for ages 6–10
- o *Zach Gets Frustrated* (Zach Rules Series) by William Mulcahy, for ages 5–8
- o *My Mouth Is a Volcano!* by Julia Cook, for ages 4 and up

At School

Children who have difficulty with shifting and flexibility are usually those kids who have a tough time transitioning between activities, especially going to nonpreferred activities. At young ages, they usually benefit from a visual schedule with several verbal reminders before the transition. They benefit significantly from a structured schedule, but will need preparation if it is necessary to change the schedule. These are the children who often have difficulty when a substitute is in the room. It is important to prepare your child for these inevitable changes by walking him or her through them, discussing feelings about them, and helping him or her determine how to handle such changes. It is probably also advisable for the teacher to alert the substitute that there are students who might need additional support. Emotionally reactive children will also require support in resolving some of the many conflicts that can erupt throughout the school day.

Consider your child. Read the examples below of how executive functioning difficulties in flexibility and emotional regulation appear in school. Do any apply to your child?

- o Gets upset if the teacher changes the way she handles the reading lesson
- o Is angry when the Internet is not working
- o Worries about a low grade on a test and can't shake off the distress
- o Gets frustrated when she cannot do a math problem and just shuts down
- o Becomes upset if she can't complete her writing assignment before time for math class
- o Cries when someone sits in her seat in the lunchroom
- o Insists on a literal interpretation of reading material and does not understand figurative language
- o Has difficulty shifting between handling different kinds of information while reading, like identifying the main idea, keeping track of characters, and making inferences
- o Has trouble shifting between addition and subtraction on a page of mixed problems
- o Has difficulty with word problems when the format changes
- o Experiences problems when shifting between different kinds of problems on tests, like moving between true/false, multiple choice, and discussion questions

At the beginning of the year, many inflexible students take a while to get accustomed to the schedule, a new teacher, and unfamiliar students. In the classroom, new learning will likely be more difficult for a child with executive functioning problems. Try to help her make the association between the new learning and something she has previously mastered. She will benefit from clear examples of what the finished product should look like since she does not handle ambiguity very well. Guided practice will help her establish a comfort level with the work, which should alleviate some anxiety.

Some suggestions for specific subject areas include:

o In language arts, work with riddles and jokes to help shift between word meanings. Explicitly teach meanings of figures of speech because inflexible children are likely to be very literal in their interpretation.

o When reading, remind them to keep in mind the different kinds of information they are seeking—character development, main idea, supporting details, and inferences.

o When creating compositions, they will benefit from a structure to follow that will make it clear that an opening, supporting details, and a closing will be required. Many schools are using story maps to facilitate organization.

o In math, students can ask themselves: Do I know another way to solve this problem, does this look similar to other problems I have seen, and is this problem the same or different from the one before it? If they are completing a page of mixed addition, subtraction, multiplication, and division problems, have them highlight signs to facilitate switching between operations.

Social Difficulties Related to Flexibility and Emotional Control

Understandably, children who are inflexible and emotionally reactive often find themselves with few friends. They likely insist on their own way and are not good at sharing. They like to call the shots when transitioning to other activities. They may not always understand the conversation because they tend to be very literal in their interpretation of language.

Talking through social situations and role-playing can help prepare them and give them practice in how to handle different scenarios. Reading stories about children and how they handle disappointments

Suggestions for Teachers

Deficits in executive functioning, like being inflexible and having poor emotional control, can significantly impact children in the classroom. We wanted to offer some suggestions that might help improve classroom functioning.

o   Never underestimate the power of a consistent, predictable routine and classroom rules.

o   Place the child close to you for ease in monitoring and cueing him.

o   Provide advance warning for changes to the schedule. For younger children, additional support from a peer or an adult may be helpful.

o   Try to help children feel that the classroom is a comfortable, safe place where learning takes place in a teacher-student partnership. Mistakes are to be expected as part of the learning process.

o   Try to make sure material is appropriate to her skill level to alleviate undue frustration.

o   Model ways to cope with change, anger, and frustration as you go throughout your day. Reframing the situation in a more positive light, problem solving about how to resolve or better the situation, or using humor to keep it in perspective can all be effective.

o   Utilize language lessons on jokes, riddles, and idioms to teach flexible thought processes.

o   During reading lessons, ask if any words have multiple meanings and then discuss them.

o   In math, encourage students to figure out more than one way to solve some problems. Have them try to recall if a presenting problem is like one they have previously solved.

Suggestions for Teachers, continued

o   Try to develop a working relationship so the student will be comfortable seeking support.

o   Be aware of triggers and warning signs that may cause the child emotional regulation difficulties. If the child appears tired, physically ill or upset, remember that his fuse could be shorter than usual.

o   Provide a space in your room where the child can go to regroup if he or she is overwhelmed. It could be a quiet reading corner or journal writing area, or just a place to sit and think for a few minutes. Teach some calming techniques, such as visualization, counting, or deep breathing.

o   Seek assistance if behavior problems are severe and do not respond to interventions.

and unexpected changes can also be instructive. Sometimes children seem to be clueless about social rules we might all take for granted, so making sure they understand expectations will be important.

Sometimes a schematic or map can be helpful in clarifying a situation where the child has become upset. In her book *Executive Function in Education: From Theory to Practice*, Meltzer (2007) used graphic organizers similar to the one in Figure 3 to help a child understand actions and outcomes.

Sometimes social stories can help the child see the situation more clearly. The concept of social stories was developed by Carol Gray to help children on the autism spectrum understand situations more clearly by describing a story like the one that happened or one very similar to what will happen. The child might be able to understand how other people in the story viewed the behavior and how effective the behavior was in resolving the situation. If you would like to use social stories, you can find many examples and learn how to create your own social stories by entering "social stories" in an Internet search engine.

In the Community

A child with difficulties in flexibility and emotional control may experience more difficulties in the community than anywhere else because it is usually less predictable and certainly not as structured as the school setting. Some of the difficulties that might occur in the community include:

o Pouts when unable to bat first at baseball or softball practice
o Runs away from you at the playground when told it is time to go
o Tantrums when not allowed to get a treat at the store
o Cannot accept a coach's decision for him to play as a defender rather than as goalie
o Refuses to eat in the restaurant when it has run out of a favorite dish

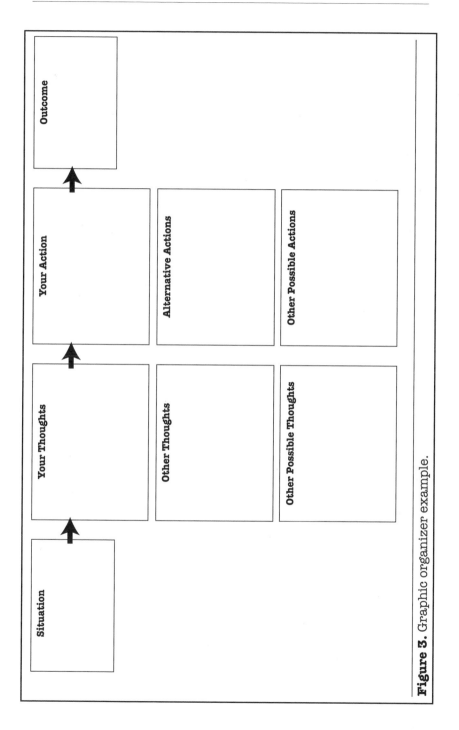

Figure 3. Graphic organizer example.

Helping Your Child's Participation in Team Sports

When you sign your child up to play a team sport, try to have him or her placed on a team with a coach who may have some understanding of how to redirect inflexible and volatile children. Remember that coaches are volunteers coming from all walks of life. Make sure to have a conversation with the coach before the first practice to let him or her know strategies that work with your child. Some coaches appreciate a short list of ideas in writing. If your child is predictably volatile, then stay for the practice in case your assistance is needed.

Talk to your child about sportsmanship—what it means and how it is demonstrated. Children often take behavioral cues from parents, so make sure your own behavior is above reproach. Sports are supposed to be a confidence builder and fun activity for children. Don't be one of those parents who yell when a child misses a ball. If time permits, role-play various situations that might come up and potential responses. Help your child understand that the coaches and umpires or referees are in charge, not the players. Things happen quickly in sports, and decisions made are not always fair.

In community activities in general, it is important to prepare your child for any changes you know about. Many times, children look forward to their participation in community events, so they can become easily disappointed at any changes or adjustments that have to be made. When weather or unexpected events cause anticipated activities to be cancelled, let your child assist in planning a follow-up activity and put it on the calendar. Community activities can facilitate building self-esteem, forging friendships, and physical development. Plan your child's activities carefully to make the most of her strengths and serve as a venue for strengthening weaker areas. That is not to say you should not encourage your child to try different activities as you help him or her find a passion.

Leveraging Strengths

If you child is goal-oriented, he or she may be very motivated to learn strategies to help handle inflexibility and intense emotions because these can interfere with reaching goals. He or she may be very open to learning mindfulness techniques like meditation or yoga to help. If the child also has good impulse control, then he or she is more likely to stop and think before exhibiting anger or frustration. Being goal-oriented and having good impulse control are definite strengths that can enable the child to stop and think about the situation in relationship to an identified goal before acting. Unfortunately, many children who are emotionally reactive are also impulsive, so helping them learn to stop and think before acting will be challenging.

Leveraging Technology

You can help your child learn to use technology to improve his or her flexibility, ability to shift to different activities, and emotional control. Below are suggested strategies for using technology:

- o A visual timer, like Time Timer, helps keep track of time remaining in a task.
- o Social stories, a concept developed by Carol Gray, can be written about specific changes the child will be facing that involve change. More information and samples can be found by putting "social stories" in a search engine.
- o Apps like Hidden Curriculum for Kids can help children learn about unwritten social "rules."
- o Schedules can be created and monitored on apps or on the computer.
- o Calming music available on a variety of devices can help some children gain emotional control more quickly.

Next Steps

After reading this chapter, take a minute for the following exercise.

An idea I can put into action is . . .

_____

_____

_____

_____

_____

_____

_____

_____

_____

_____

_____

_____

_____

_____

_____

_____

CHAPTER 6

Focusing and Self-Monitoring

"Life is like a camera
Focus on what is important
Capture the good times
Develop from the negatives
And if things don't work out, take another shot."
—Unknown

Self-Reflection Survey

1. How often do you start projects without completing them?
   a. Most of the time. I have great intentions, but not a lot of follow-through.
   b. Some of the time. If I stay interested I can finish. Otherwise, I don't.
   c. Not very often. I almost always get the job done.

2. How long is your child able to focus on a task she doesn't really like to do?
   a. If she doesn't like the task, she can't even focus enough to start.
   b. A few minutes, but she usually needs several reminders.
   c. She rushes through the job without doing it well or completely.
   d. She completes it competently with few or no reminders.

3. If I point out that my child's work contains several errors or omissions, he is:
   a. surprised
   b. ashamed
   c. grateful for the help
   d. argumentative

4. My child is able to pick out key concepts from a story or lesson.
   a. all the time
   b. most of the time
   c. some of the time
   d. rarely

5. Describe homework time at your house:
   a. It's a nightmare.
   b. It's difficult but manageable.
   c. It takes forever.
   d. It's a lovely time of day during which my child works quietly, independently, and efficiently, and I am able to relax, put my feet up, and enjoy a refreshing beverage and a good book. (You're allowed to laugh. It doesn't happen this way at our houses either.)

Is It a Focusing or Self-Monitoring Problem?

How do you know if your child has difficulty with focusing and self-monitoring? If the behaviors below describe your child, then you are in the right area.

o   Can't pay attention long enough to grasp and follow instructions

o Doesn't appear to be listening when spoken to
o Changes from one task to another without completing any
o Has a hard time staying focused on the task if he isn't extremely motivated or he hyper-focuses on activities of great interest
o Has problems concentrating
o Procrastinates
o Daydreams
o Can be easily distracted by surroundings, sounds, and other stimuli
o Starts a lot of projects, but has difficulty finishing any
o Makes careless mistakes in schoolwork, chores, and other activities
o Has a difficult time accepting and applying constructive criticism or seeing where his shortcomings lie
o Has difficulty seeing how his behavior or actions affect others

If your child's executive functioning difficulties manifest as difficulty with focusing on tasks, consider the strategies in this chapter to help at home, in school, and in the community.

What Does Focusing and Self-Monitoring Mean?

These two executive functions are interrelated:
o *Focus*: The ability to pay attention to instructions, apply what you know to a problem or situation, and concentrate on the work through to completion; and
o *Self-monitoring*: The ability to oversee your own behavior and activity in an objective way, making needed adjustments and corrections that lead to the successful outcome of a task, chore, or situation.

As children grow, they learn to process, evaluate, and act on the vast amount of information that surrounds them at all times. At some point, we all had to learn what kinds of information we needed to pay attention to and what we could ignore. As a child, you might have learned the hard way that it wasn't a great idea to pay undivided attention to *Tom & Jerry* when Mom was trying to call you for dinner or get you to clean your room. Focus is what allows us to mentally select the information that's important and relevant, and then transition into acting on that information from beginning to end. Focus is the act of paying attention to what we're doing, avoiding the urge to become distracted or called away to something we find more interesting or diverting. Think of it as the growth of mental muscle power.

As your child grows and matures, he'll face ever-increasing responsibilities. You're well aware that not everything an adult is asked to do in a day is stimulating, but a lot of it just needs to get done. Focus is the skill that allows us to work through all tasks, whether interesting or mundane. Focus is also the skill that allows us to learn and grow in all realms of life. We can't learn and retain anything—whether it's a fact, a skill, or a task—without having paid attention to it in the first place.

> *Focus is the skill that allows us to work through all tasks, whether interesting or mundane.*

As an extension of this, the ability to self-monitor is almost a special kind of focus, allowing us to constantly review our own actions and make large or small adjustments, as necessary, for the best possible result. Your child will take a lot of his cues on this from you. If you are open-minded to constructive criticism or suggestions about how you might improve, then it's likely your child will be also. If you are willing to consider your performance objectively and see what's working well and what isn't, then you teach that skill to your child. If you realize that your behavior affects others in a way that's harmful to relationships, then your child may witness your attempts to try a different approach in the future. Self-monitoring is the little internal voice that first asks, "How am I doing?" and then gives the answer.

Developmental Context

If you watch a baby play with his toes, you'd almost think that the ability to focus came hardwired in humans. Ten toes, 10 minutes of complete, uninterrupted fascination. But focus requires intent and an understanding that the world delivers lots of information and it's our job to be able to sort it all out. All Kinds of Minds is a New Hampshire-based organization that supports teachers and parents of kids who learn differently. It uses the term *saliency determination*, which describes the ability to select incoming information that is most important to the task at hand while simultaneously rejecting unrelated information and avoiding distractions (All Kinds of Minds, 2014). That's the kind of focus we need our kids to develop.

When a child has trouble focusing, it sometimes comes off as laziness, lack of concern, or limited intelligence. There's a temptation to think a child isn't the brightest bulb in the fixture if his mind often wanders, or if he forgets a set of instructions mere seconds after they've been offered. Please, resist this temptation. If this is your quietly held opinion of an otherwise bright and engaged child, you'll telegraph this perception whether you realize it or not.

The big (although often unspoken) question for most parents is, "How can I teach my child to focus/behave/remember?" but it should be this one: "How is my child going to turn out?" Today, wherever you are in your child's journey toward independence, remember there are a lot of days before his thinking and abilities are fully formed. There's lots of time, and you can have lots of influence. This is one area in which you cannot do the work for him. You cannot get in his head and force focus; you can simply show him what it looks like and help him develop the skills bit by bit. You cannot pipe your voice into his head to prompt that internal dialogue that lets him assess and adjust; you just keep walking alongside him, asking questions and gently pointing out his options.

Meanwhile, as you consider your child's progress on the mastery of focus and self-monitoring, it's important to recognize that lack of focus can be prompted by a number of other factors unrelated to neurological development. In our practices, we remind parents to rule out the following factors that mimic a diminished ability to focus:

- o   poor sleep or insufficient sleep,
- o   inadequate nutrition,
- o   vitamin deficiency,
- o   vision problems,
- o   hearing impairment,
- o   slow cognitive processing speed, and
- o   lack of physical exercise.

Also, please understand that simply because your child may exhibit signs of focus or self-monitoring challenges, it does not necessarily mean he has ADHD. Executive functioning difficulty occurs alone or with other disorders including ADHD, learning disabilities, emotional disorders, and autism spectrum disorders.

The development of language skills in a child is a key component in the art of self-monitoring. A child's own words guide his behavior. Think about it: You automatically use inner language to help yourself focus and pay attention, even if you're not highly interested in a task. Sure, you may do some things on autopilot, especially mundane chores that you've done hundreds of thousands of time. But there's still an inner voice that keeps you on task from start to finish, or you'd have your washer and dryer and dishwasher and vacuum and leaf blower and lawnmower and hot glue gun and television and garden hose and shower all going at the same time. If you *do* regularly have your washer and dryer and dishwasher and vacuum and leaf blower and lawnmower and hot glue gun and television and garden hose and shower all going at the same time, you may

A child's own words guide his behavior.

want to think about what habits you're modeling for your child.

Table 4 includes the guidelines for the development of focus and self-monitoring skills.

Table 4. *Guidelines for Focus and Self-Monitoring Development*

Ages 4–5	■ Able to start and complete simple chores of 5 minutes or less. ("Pick up your stuffed animals and put them in your toy box.") ■ Able to pay attention for a short book, song, or brief game. Able to focus longer on subjects and activities of great interest.
Ages 6–8	■ Can follow a series of instructions with three separate parts. ■ Able to focus on a task for 15–30 minutes. ■ Concentrates on longer reading passages and is able to pick out key points.
Ages 9–12	■ Able to focus on a task for an hour or more. ■ Can follow a series of instructions with five or more separate parts. ■ Can focus on more than one thing at once.

In the Home

In teaching focus and self-monitoring, we want to emphasize that how you speak to your child is just as important as what you say to her. In all likelihood, she may be aware that she seems a little spacier than her friends, and she's worried by it. She fears she's stupid because it's so hard for her to concentrate. There are a number of gentle techniques you can use to communicate with her, always guiding her back to clear focus on her task or chore.

We consistently hear parents lament that their child not only has difficulty starting a task, but can't seem to stay with it and often completes it sloppily or leaves part of it undone altogether. You might ask your child to straighten up her backpack, but an hour later either (a) she hasn't touched it; (b) she's done the large compartment but not the smaller pockets; (c) she's taken everything out, but hasn't sorted or organized it; or (d) she says she's done it, but it looks (to you) just as messy and disorganized as it did before. What to do?

People who struggle to initiate a project and stay focused on it tend to need a lot of structure as they approach the endeavor. We find the following steps helpful for most children and adults with focus difficulties:

1. First, outline everything the project or task entails, using a checklist if necessary. Remember, one of the reasons your child may not start is that she can't get a grasp on everything the project requires or in what order things need to be done. With an older child, you may be able to talk through all of the steps as he writes out the checklist. A younger child may need a picture list illustrating each step.

2. Discuss the time frame. This includes when the child is expected to start, how long each part of the task will probably take, and what time he or she should strive to finish. As much as possible, try to tie the completion of the project to some sort of consequence that provides motivation. "You have 20 minutes of spelling homework and 20 minutes of math homework. If you start now and take a short break in between, you can be done by 5:30 and we'll be able to take a bike ride together before dinner." Be sure to keep your word.

3. Realize that in the beginning, you will have to gently redirect your child back to the task at hand. To continue the above example, you can expect that your child will break away from her spelling homework after 10 minutes to report that there is a red cardinal on the birdfeeder. Without acknowledging the distraction, guide her back to the work area and use the word "focus," as in, "Please remember that your focus right now is on your spelling work."

4. Especially with younger children, plan to stay nearby. We all work better when there's a chance the boss might walk into the room. Without sitting directly next to her and watching her every move, you'll be able to get a good sense of whether she's on track or not.

5. When (note we did not say "if") you notice your child is losing focus before completing the task, take the opportunity to review what she's already done before setting her back on track. "I'm really glad to see you got your spelling homework done, and that you came right back to the table after your 10-minute break. And you've already done three math prob-

lems. The finish line is in sight! You only have 15 more minutes and you'll be all done."

6. When she indicates she's finished, review her work. Children with focus problems often don't notice if they've skipped over problems or left certain parts of the project undone. Ask her to check her own work as if she's her teacher, parent, or other objective person. If there are mistakes or omissions, but she's still unable to recognize them, spell them out as nonjudgmentally as possible.

7. When she's done, she's earned your genuine praise. Remember, staying focused takes a lot of energy for your child, far more than you might expect. So not only did she expend the energy to do the actual task, she worked just as hard to keep her mind on the job.

Here's a trick we like. You know that even as adults, we sometimes find ourselves having trouble getting started on a project or maintaining focus. Set a timer for what seems like a very short time—for an adult, it could be 20 minutes; for an older child, 10–15 minutes; for a young child, 5 minutes. Pledge that you will work with focus for the entire time, and that when the timer goes off, you can quit for a while. An interesting thing seems to happen. Because we know we don't have much time, we work efficiently and get more done than we ever thought possible. And a lot of the time, when the timer goes off, we've built up enough momentum that we don't feel like stopping.

Ways to Help Younger Children

Your young child needs a bit of extra guidance. You might scaffold support by sitting beside her at homework time and reading a book or doing some paperwork. Having you there will help keep her on track, and she'll see you doing some focused work of your own.

As she's learning to complete tasks, having her read directions aloud (or reading the directions to her) can be beneficial. If it's permitted, have her circle important words on her worksheet. Because she struggles to know what information is important, that visual clue can serve as a reminder of what she's meant to focus on.

Also, making a game of tasks, especially boring or distasteful ones, can be another way to make time fly and help your child stay focused. If it's time to clean up his room, you can challenge your 5-year-old to a race. Tell him you'll put away everything on his bed, but he'll have to clean up the floor. It's a fun way to teach him a lot of focus-related lessons. First, you'll be in the same room and he'll see you working with single-minded focus. Second, because he's racing you, he will use his time efficiently or risk losing. Finally, when he's finished the task and had fun doing it, you can point out how well he was able to keep on task. He'll have an immediate recognition of what it felt like, and with practice he may be able to work that way on his own.

Ways to Help Older Children

Our young people live in a world full of flashy, fun, sparkly distractions. Kids love to multitask, but for them it means having TV and music on at the same time they're texting their friends and playing a video game. It's chaos. One of the biggest breaks you can give a kid with focus problems is to get rid of the distractions. Don't have the television on watching your own show if you're expecting your child to be in the same room doing her homework. But we do sometimes find that playing soft, relaxing music as background noise can filter out other distractions and help a child concentrate.

One of the biggest breaks you can give a kid with focus problems is to get rid of the distractions.

Distractions happen everywhere, not just while doing schoolwork. If you've asked your child to rake the leaves, it's reasonable to let her listen to music on her headphones. But if you notice she's sitting on the porch talking on her cellphone, you're going to want to remind her where her focus belongs and let her figure out how to handle the distraction of the phone. Should she let it go to voicemail? Talk on a headset while she does her chore? Put the phone inside the house?

Books for Children

Consider reading the following books with your child to reinforce his ability to learn to focus and monitor. Follow the framework outlined in previous chapters, which included: (a) read the book ahead of time to make sure it's appropriate; (b) read to or with your child and pause to discuss the book's ideas; (c) discuss how the book's character used the skill or solved a problem; and (d) discuss how the ideas can help in your family or at school.

- *I Just Want To Do It My Way: My Story About Staying on Task and Asking for Help* (Best Me I Can Be!) by Julia Cook, for ages 5–12
- *Learning to Slow Down & Pay Attention: A Book for Kids About ADHD* by Kathleen G. Nadeau, for ages 4 and up

At School

Shelly is a 5-year-old kindergarten student who is very social and loves talking to her peers. Shelly is helpful and likes to assist the teacher whenever she can. In the classroom, Shelly is fine as long as there is no change. Shelly likes to be in control; she does not like to be told what to do. This behavior poses a problem because she often wanders off and does what she wants in the classroom.

Shelly's teacher often talks to Shelly about focusing on the task at hand. During read-aloud time, Shelly often leaves the group to play on the computer. The teacher's assistant usually walks over to Shelly and asks her to return to the group. Shelly returns but she starts playing with her hair or shoes and does not pay attention to what the teacher is saying. Shelly's teacher came up with a technique to reward her every time she focuses for at least 5 minutes on the task at hand and does not get distracted by her surroundings. Shelly is given extra computer time after she focuses and completes her task.

Here are some signs your child has focus or monitoring challenges in the classroom:

o Can't concentrate long enough to learn the alphabet or numbers
o Difficulty waiting for her turn in group activities
o Does not begin or complete homework without supervision
o Packs, but forgets essential items
o Reads the problem but can't break it into understandable parts
o Has problems grasping rules of a game and functioning as a team player
o Has to read through texts repeatedly to understand
o Struggles with completing tasks, especially multistep tasks
o When called on, forgets what he was planning to say
o Daydreams in situations when he is expected to listen
o Often fidgets and becomes restless or bored in situations that require focus and concentration

Can you imagine how draining school can be for a child who struggles with executive functions—particularly focus issues?

There is one primary reason to maintain focus at school: You cannot learn and build on information if that information has bounced right off you in the first place. Focus is all about the management and absorption of information, the weeding out of what's unimportant and the retention of what is valuable. As a child grows, he'll be asked to build upon his store of knowledge and experience. In first grade, he needs to be able to focus on and retain the first grade stuff. That's so he'll be able to build on that the following year and so on. The more he loses focus, the harder it will be for him to catch up later and the more discouraged he may feel.

> *There is one primary reason to maintain focus at school: You cannot learn and build on information if that information has bounced right off you in the first place.*

Schools provide a lot of the structure required for people with focus problems, and teachers are adept at dividing the school day into age-appropriate blocks of time for activities and lessons—long enough to teach and learn, but not so long that children get restless and tune out. But your child has lower-than-average ability to focus. How's he going to make it through the day?

One way is to start to develop his awareness of the times he's drifting off. He can wear a watch-like device (one common device is called the WatchMinder) that vibrates randomly and/or displays a preprogrammed message like "pay attention." That provides an opportunity for him to self-check: Was I tuned in or tuned out just then? Often, he's not the only child in class who tends to lose focus. Some teachers, especially those with younger students, like to do an "attention pop quiz" at random times of the day. It may be very valuable to make this a whole-class exercise, so that one or two children don't feel singled out in this area.

You and your child can also talk about what it feels like to lose focus, how easily it happens, and the ways it affects his relationship with his teacher and his classmates. You might suggest your child answer the question, "What do I do that shows I'm paying attention?" You can talk about the different behaviors that go along with focus, and maybe make a reminder sheet to tape to your child's desk or to a notebook. Here are some focus-enhancing behaviors you and your child can work on:

- I make sure to look at the teacher while he or she is teaching or speaking.
- When a classmate is answering a question or presenting a report, I look at him or her.
- I make eye contact with my teacher when I'm asked a question.
- I know the kinds of things that distract me, and so I keep any distracting items put away in my desk or in my backpack. (Work with your child to find out what he fiddles with and what draws his attention away. Sometimes it can be very effective to have *one* designated item, like a stress ball, that he's allowed to manipulate while he's listening. The mere act of touching the ball acts as a reminder to pay attention.)
- I know the times of day I tend to lose focus. Sometimes this is because I'm hungry, so I can ask for special permission to have a healthy snack right around this time of the day.

○ I am aware of special phrases my teacher uses to indicate that information is important. I take note when he or she says, "You will need to know this for the test," or "We will cover three important concepts in today's class."

Ways to Help Younger Children at School

When they first start school, little children often are eager to show what they've learned. Even a child with a focus problem can bring home some new tidbit, like how to tie her shoes or the rules to a new game. Be sure to praise what she has learned, rather than emphasize the areas that are troublesome. Eventually, she *will* learn the alphabet; she'll just need more practice than some of her classmates. Eventually, she *will* learn to read. Eventually, she *will* be able to count from 1 to 100. For a child who has difficulty focusing, it's a big deal to remember how to get from 1–10, and then from 1–20. Celebrate the triumphs along the way.

A Harvard University study determined that focus and planning skills can be developed and improved even when a child is in preschool. The study examined two sets of students—one group that was taught a purely academic curriculum of math, science, and language and a second group that was also given instruction in executive function skills, such as private self-talk. Children who were exposed to that curriculum not only improved in the areas of focus, planning, and other executive functions, but they made greater strides academically (Diamond, Barnett, Thomas, & Munro, 2007). Here's the encouragement we want to offer: The work you do with your child to help her focus is very likely to have other benefits as well.

Also, it's a great idea to talk with your kids about the other children in the room, and which of their friends tend to be distracting. When they have a choice, suggest that they look around and see who's sitting next to them. Teach them to ask themselves, "Will I be too tempted to talk to the person next to me? Should I move to a different spot so I'll be able to concentrate on my work?" Your child can learn to make such a move in a quiet and subtle way so he doesn't hurt anyone's feelings, but it's likely you'll need to work with him on that part as well or ask his teacher to help.

Ways to Help Older Children at School

As children move into the middle school years, the ability to focus often improves slightly. The problem is that the amount of information coming at them increases dramatically, and they may feel even less able to cope than before.

In her book *Promoting Executive Function in the Classroom*, Dr. Lynn Meltzer (2010) described what she and colleague Kalyani Krishnan have deemed "the funnel model." Students with EF experience an overload of information, so there's more going in than there is coming out. "Because these students cannot process this information rapidly enough and cannot shift approaches flexibly, they cannot easily unclog the funnel to produce finished work" (Meltzer, 2010, p. 9).

So your middle schooler is using much of his time and energy just trying to keep up with the onslaught of information coming at him. His head (the funnel) is just jammed with it. So when he finally does produce a piece of work, there's a great likelihood that he's not able to see whether that work meets the basic standards most teachers will expect. He may skip over problems or forget to do portions of written assignments or be unable to effectively check over math assignments or proofread his written work. This moves beyond focus and into the area of self-monitoring. Because processing the information and doing the work has required so much effort, Meltzer (2010) noted, "[students] have trouble shifting to a self-checking mindset, and do not stop to look for possible errors and to revise their work" (p. 163).

We find the following strategies can be helpful as older children try to manage a great deal of information and then present it in an acceptable form:

o   Ask the teacher for a copy of lecture notes that can be taken home to review pertinent points.

o   Work with your child so that she begins to recognize areas where she tends to slip up. She needs to realize you're not doing this to find fault, but help her avoid the kinds of pitfalls that have been costly in the past. Maybe she frequently leaves blank spaces on her math worksheets, for example. Have her go over every single problem, touching each with her fingertip to make sure she's recorded an answer. She can do this on tests too to make sure she answers every question.

o   If proofreading written work is a problem, have him read his composition out loud. Every word, slowly, exactly as he's written it. For many people it's easier to recognize a mistake that sounds funny than it is to see it on the page.

o   Teach your child how to make outlines for large projects. Your child may use an outline to map out the steps to a science project, not only to help get her brain around all of the steps involved, but to help her figure out what to do first, second, third, etc. Once she breaks a large project into plenty of pieces, she may be better able to picture herself focusing on one or two small pieces per day.

o   Similarly, outlines are crucial for longer written reports and essays. You may work with your child's teacher to ask him or her to review your child's outline before he begins writing, to make sure he has covered all of the salient points. Referring to the outline during the writing process will help keep him on track as well. Suggest that he focus on one section at a time, and then when his focus wanes, take a break. He'll come back to the next section refreshed, but the flow of the work will still make sense. The outline will also help him make sure he doesn't over focus on any one particular area.

In the Community

Just like your child may have trouble noticing and correcting errors in schoolwork and chores, she may fail to notice when she's behaving in a way that's not socially acceptable. A child may rattle on and on about an area of profound interest to her, not noticing that her friend's eyes have glazed over. She may be so immersed in a cartoon she's drawing that she fails to realize her teacher has spoken sharply to

Suggestions for Teachers

Deficits in executive functioning, like having difficulty focusing, can significantly impact children in the classroom. We wanted to offer some suggestions that might help improve classroom functioning.

- We like to teach focus in baby steps. Ask your students to work diligently at a task for 3 minutes. No bathroom breaks, no questions, no talking. Afterward, talk about focus and what it means, and ask if it was easy or difficult for her. Work into longer and longer sessions, and suggest she practice at home. Make it part of a homework assignment not only to complete the work, but also to do it in one uninterrupted sitting.

- Although some students have more focus issues than others, most children need reinforcement in this area. When possible, make focus-related instruction a whole-class activity. Stage regular "attention pop quizzes." Stop what you're doing and, in the same tone of voice, say, "If you're paying attention, raise your hand." Have a small reward for those children who succeed, but don't penalize those who don't. The idea is to bring awareness and develop the skill, not shame the children whose minds tend to wander.

- Help students learn how to review their own work and to shift from the "doer" to the "checker." You might create and distribute laminated "checker cards" for various subjects. The cards would list common things students forget ("Is my name on the paper?" and "Did I answer all the questions?") and also subject-specific reminders ("Have I left out or misspelled words in my essay?" or "Did I remember to include remainders?").

- Let there be a benefit for reviewing work and catching errors. It's important for students with self-monitoring challenges to have an incentive to learn to check and correct their own work.

Suggestions for Teachers, continued

- o Precise language helps students grasp the main ideas of a lesson. (For example, "We will cover four main points today.") When possible, hand out an outline or lecture notes students can review later.

- o Try playing soft background music or white noise in your classroom to help students filter out distracting sounds around them, both from within the classroom and outside.

- o Be mindful of where students are placed in the classroom, and find the spots that make sense for each child. We tend to place students with focus problems near the front of the room, but that doesn't always work for all kids.

- o Children with focus challenges may need reduced workloads.

- o See if you can develop a wide repertoire of nonverbal reminders to help students whose minds wander. Walk over and stand right beside them as you're teaching. Place a light hand on their shoulder. Develop a little reminder gesture just between you and that one unfocused student who needs extra help.

- o Finally, emphasize to your students that everybody goofs off and lets their mind wander from time to time. The key to growing and maturing is to learn to control *when* you let your mind wander and for how long and to develop the ability to draw your attention back to the task at hand.

her three or four times. She may get in trouble at soccer practice or at Sunday school, and genuinely have no idea why.

This tends to go back to the challenges she has with self-monitoring, or the ability to review her conduct from an objective point of view and make constant adjustments. In the case of her poor bored friend, she's so focused on her own area of interest that she can't realize her friend doesn't share her enthusiasm. Here are some ways you can help your child grow in this area:

- o It's helpful for a child with self-monitoring challenges to get a little help recognizing body language and facial expressions. Review photos of people expressing a variety of different emotions and projecting many different sorts of body language. Talk through the different emotions she observes, and help clue her in to any she might have missed.

- o Similarly, help her become more fluent in understanding someone's tone of voice. You can have some fun mimicking happy people, sad people, impatient people, and frustrated people. When she begins to be able to recognize the emotions of the people around her, she may start to be able to adjust her own behavior accordingly.

- o If friends, teammates, or neighbors tend to react to your child in a way she finds upsetting, talk through the situation. Ask her to describe the situation as if she were a "fly on the wall" or someone who'd never met any of the participants before. Help her understand any ways she might have behaved differently, and how the outcome may have been different.

Leveraging Strengths

If your child has working memory strengths, you can teach him to use his strong memory to increase focusing and self-monitoring. Your child can remember to "check himself" periodically throughout his lessons and ask, "Am I paying attention?" Some parents give their child a personalized pencil with a message such as, "Am I paying attention?" or "Keep working hard." This discrete visual helps children remember to self-monitor and increase focus.

Leveraging Technology

Technology in this area is still developing. We've already mentioned the WatchMinder as a tool to bring awareness to a child's level of focus. If your child is old enough to have a smartphone, then you can send a text at a designated time to remind your child to focus on turning in his or her homework or writing down all assignments from the board. Some parents set reminders on their child's phone to receive a notice at the end of the day to bring home all required materials for completing homework.

Next Steps

After reading this chapter, take a minute for the following exercise.

An idea I can put into action is . . .

_____

_____

_____

_____

_____

_____

_____

_____

_____

_____

_____

_____

CHAPTER 7

Not Just Ordinary Organizing

"You'll never change your life until you change something you do daily. The secret to your success is found in your daily routine."—John C. Maxwell

Self-Reflection Survey

1. I rate my ability to organize my child's life as:
   a. low
   b. medium
   c. high
   d. does not apply

2. My child's current organizational skills are causing problems in school or home.
   a. yes
   b. no
   c. somewhat
   d. does not apply

3. My child's ability to organize his or her belongings or materials is:
   a. low
   b. medium
   c. high
   d. developing

4. I believe my child should learn to create his or her own organizational system.
   a. yes
   b. no
   c. does not apply

5. I am aware of technology tools to help my child learn to organize.
   a. yes
   b. no
   c. somewhat
   d. does not apply

Is This a Problem?

How do you know if your child has difficulty with organizing? If the behaviors below describe your child then you are in the right chapter.

- o Cluttered workspace
- o Messy backpack
- o Clothes all over the floor
- o Dishes and food wrappers under the bed
- o Homework completed but not turned in for credit
- o Doesn't know due dates
- o Can't locate materials

What Is It?

In the context of this chapter, when we refer to organization skills, we refer to your child's ability to organize *stuff*. (We'll go into more details about organizing information, thoughts, and ideas in Chapter 11: Planning, Setting Goals, and Using Critical Thinking). We think of organizing skill as the ability to impose order on tools, equipment, other possessions, and storage.

It's pretty obvious that a child isn't going to be able to succeed on a higher level if he can't ever find a pencil and a piece of paper when he has a good idea. If we can figure out how to help him keep his possessions, school supplies, and sports gear organized, then he has a fair shake at succeeding in the other areas of life.

"Aha!" you might be saying. "My child's focus, working memory, and impulse-control issues are going to take a lot of time and patience and practice for him to show improvement. But I can get him organized right now!" And you could.

You could go right out to an office supply superstore and buy your child a planner, a set of color-coordinated folders, and an array of highlighters and labels for every conceivable purpose. While you're there, make sure to pick up one of those huge vinyl wall calendars, so your child can keep track of every appointment, project, practice, and game. Why not even stop by the Apple store and buy your child an iPhone? He'll be thrilled, and you know the calendar app on *your* phone helps keep you on track. Then it's off to the home furnishing store for storage crates and cubbies and organizer bins for all of the toys, games, and miscellaneous nonsense kids seem to drag home by the ton. Finally, stop at the home supply store so you can outfit your garage with a state-of-the-art sports gear rack. A place for everything, and everything in its place.

Not so fast. It's not that any of those ideas are bad ones or wrong. You've read all of them before, and some of them might work very well for your family. But here's the key: The organizing system that works for *you* may not help *your child* one bit. One mom we know spent hours painstakingly sorting her son's loose LEGO pieces into a dozen different compartmentalized boxes according to size and function. The problem? Her son didn't have the slightest bit of interest in having his LEGOs categorized. (Would you?) So her system fell apart within a week. The best organizing system for your child is one you create together, experiment with, and refine. He may need to try a few different approaches until he finds one that he's able to manage with consistency.

Developmental Context

Like many other executive functioning difficulties, the inability to organize possessions is considered a developmental weakness, so your child's organizational difficulty can't be directly linked to a specific cause. But you already know that some executive functioning difficulties tend to have a genetic component, in that they may be passed down from one generation to the next. Are you disorganized? Your child's disorganization may be a function of heredity, or he may simply be reflecting the environment in which he is being raised. Or both. It may be obvious, but as a parent, you can't alter the rate at which your child's brain develops. But you can have a dramatic impact on the environment in which he lives.

It's important for your child to understand that organizational abilities have very little to do with intelligence—but that *lack* of organizational abilities can make it harder for him to succeed at school and in life. We all know plenty of very bright adults who can be tremendously scattered. Unlike some other executive functioning difficulties, organizational challenges may be simply a matter of personality. Some folks thrive on neatness and order, and others are unbothered by clutter and chaos.

As you are helping your child develop his own organizational skills, remember that the more demanding the task, the more help he may need. Organization skills research suggests that it's important to master one skill before moving onto the next. "Schema theory suggests that individuals process complex situations by using their previously encoded general knowledge about similar situations" (Meltzer, 2010, p. 89). So before your preteen is able to grasp everything that goes into organizing his backpack for school, he may just need to work on a system for papers that need to be signed and returned. Before your 6-year-old is able to put all her

> *It's important for your child to understand that organizational abilities have very little to do with intelligence—but that lack of organizational abilities can make it harder for him to succeed at school and in life.*

Table 5. Guidelines for Organizational Skill Development

Ages 4–5	■ Typically enjoy making a game of tidying up, and recognize that most objects have a proper place. ■ Understand that "like" items are stored together. (For example, socks go in pairs in one drawer, shirts in another.)
Ages 6–8	■ May have tendency for hoarding. Able to create special settings for their collections. ■ Understand the value of maintaining an organized school backpack or desk, but still need help accomplishing this.
Ages 9–12	■ Able to help establish their own practices for organizing their possessions. Should be able to make decisions about what's worth keeping. On the upper end of this age range, can become involved in the care of their own possessions (like maintaining sports equipment or doing their own laundry).

toys away, she may need to learn how to separate the blocks from the cuddle toys and the art supplies. As much as possible, break down the bigger task into logical steps. Make sure your child is comfortable with each step along the way, and only then have her move on.

Table 5 includes the guidelines for the development of organizational skills in children.

In the Home

A big part of helping your child get organized when he's at home will revolve around establishing routines and good habits. Kids with EF difficulties need lots of repetition. Repeating behaviors leads to establishing habits, whether they're good habits or bad habits.

If your kids are anything like our kids, a lot of the time they just want to know the "why" of the thing—in this case, why they have to take the time to organize themselves and their possessions. There are lots of reasons, from efficiency at homework time, to having a clean and safe living environment, to being able to find their favorite toy when they want it. At home, organizational challenges affect two major areas: homework and a child's living space.

Let's talk about homework first. "A common complaint of many children is that they don't have time to do the things they want to do" because their homework is so time-consuming, wrote Kalyani Krishnan and her colleague, Dr. Lynn Meltzer (2014, para. 13). As the parent, you can encourage and motivate your child when you emphasize that the *reason* you want to help him become an organized person is that having a system will make his life easier. Remember, he thinks that organization is hard. You must show him there's a payoff in the end:

A big part of helping your child get organized when he's at home will revolve around establishing routines and good habits.

- o Your homework goes more smoothly.
- o You have more time for other things.
- o You feel less stress and pressure.
- o When your school materials are organized, you can finish faster and have time for the things you want to do. You don't need to spend an hour rounding up all of the necessary items before you even start. Who wants to spend an hour hunting for a pencil and looking for a worksheet when you could be climbing trees or drawing pictures or listening to music?

You probably already know the value of designating a quiet, clutter-free, distraction-free area for your child to do schoolwork. For younger children, it's especially helpful to have a "homework box" that contains pencils, pens, erasers, lined paper—whatever supplies your child regularly needs at homework time. Help her understand that it's her responsibility to get the box out, lay out the items she'll need that day, replace them when her homework is done, and return the box to its proper place. Not only does this help reduce the amount of time she spends looking for the tools she needs to complete her work, every time she uses the box she's getting practice with the concepts behind organization, including:

- o gathering all necessary items for a task,
- o maintaining those items,

○ replacing and replenishing as necessary, and

○ returning the items to their proper storage location.

Older children can use this system successfully as well. Many pre-teens have their own desk in their bedrooms, but we all know how hard it is to keep a desk organized. It's much easier to organize one box or drawer. The desk can come later, and for some of us, it never really comes at all.

When it comes to helping your child with his room, don't assume for a minute he has any idea of how to organize the space. Start small. Take your child on a tour of your own bedroom and show him how you've decided to arrange it, and why. Explain everything, from why you put your wallet in your sock drawer ("I always know how to find it, and it's out of sight") to why the bathroom towels go in the bathroom linen closet ("You put towels close to where you need them"). Take a tour through other areas of the house, and talk about other organizational systems. Your keys and sunglasses always go in the same spot. Why? So you never have to hunt for them. What spot doesn't matter, as long as it's meaningful to *you*. Ask your child if he has any suggestions for how your home may be better organized, and consider implementing some of his ideas. It's a powerful thing when a kid gets the chance to instruct an adult. Be willing to be taught by your child, if organization is also a challenge for you.

Now, tour your child's bedroom and/or bathroom. Talk about making the space functional for him—after all, that's the point of organization. Go through each drawer, being willing to rearrange them if he feels he's better able to manage a different setup. No point in insisting the socks go in the upper left hand drawer if he wants them in a lower drawer because they're closer to his feet.

Remind your child that a neat room and an organized room are not necessarily the same thing. If his space appears to be tidy but he still can't find anything because everything he owns is shoved into drawers and under the bed, it's not organized. By the same token, if his room looks messy to you but makes sense to him and allows him to find what he needs, he's found a functional system.

Take things slowly. Here are a couple of suggestions:

o Most children enjoy collections. Managing their collections gives them great practice in thinking through how it will be organized, displayed, and stored. It doesn't seem like work, because they collect stuff they're interested in.

o Assign your children household chores that remind them everything has its place. Young children may help you put away laundry or sort the mail. Older children could empty the dishwasher, which will help them see how your kitchen is organized and get them in the habit of putting things back in the same place every time.

There's an obvious area of overlap between home and school as it relates to your child's homework, backpack, and other school-related items like gym clothes and uniforms. Every child forgets her lunch once in a while. Without a daily reminder, we're guessing it would be an everyday occurrence for your child.

Books for Children

The following are books you can read with your child to reinforce strategies for teaching organization. Follow the framework outlined in previous chapters, which included: (a) read the book ahead of time to make sure it's appropriate; (b) read to or with your child and pause to discuss the book's ideas; (c) discuss how the book's character used the skill or solved a problem; and (d) discuss how the ideas can help in your family or at school.

o *Get Organized Without Losing It* by Janet S. Fox, for ages 8–13

o *Wyatt the Wonder Dog Learns About Being Organized* by Lynne Watts, for ages 5 and older

o *Annie's Plan: Taking Charge of Schoolwork and Homework* by Jeanne R. Kraus, for ages 7 and older

At School

Because most classroom settings are very structured, there's a lot of built-in organization in your child's school day. That's the good news. The bad news is that she's probably had no input in creating the systems that keep a classroom in order, and they may make little sense to her. If children can understand that most organizational processes are meant to help them in the long run, they may be more open and receptive to them.

Strategies for Younger Students

Four- and five-year-olds are just beginning to grasp the concept of organizing their possessions, and they need a lot of reminders. Especially during the first half of the school year, you may need to walk your kindergartner to class every day (if allowed), and remind him where to put his coat, his lunch, and his backpack. Remember, we're not presuming that he understands how to organize himself or why. These activities may help his growth in this area:

- Draw a picture of his classroom, or if he's artistic, ask him to draw it. Together, depict and label the areas related to organization—where certain toys are kept, where homework papers go. Discuss why his teacher has chosen to order the classroom this way.

- Have an afterschool visit with the teacher, and together, discuss how the room is arranged and how that helps students in the learning process.

- Give your child a responsibility related to organizing his school gear. Place the different parts of his lunch on the counter, but make him responsible for putting them properly into his lunchbox. When he's mastered that, add a second step (putting the lunchbox into the backpack).

- Pictures help young children understand organizational processes. Most students have a pencil box to hold their crayons, markers, and other writing tools. You might take the step of taping photos of those items to the top of your child's box, to help him remember what goes in it when he's at school.

Strategies for Older Students

As a child matures, her ability to organize schoolwork and school supplies begins to have a direct correlation to her ability to do her work. Think of all of the things your child needs to keep track of—worksheets and books and notebooks and completed work and reports and review sheets and folders and lunchbox and water bottle and pencils and erasers and calculators and planners. It's a lot.

> *As a child matures, her ability to organize schoolwork and school supplies begins to have a direct correlation to her ability to do her work.*

It's a lot of paper, too, and the disorganized student tends to bring home wads of crumpled-up papers. Some need your signature and must be returned to the teacher. Others describe a science project that's due in 2 weeks. Some of them will be her doodles and drawings. Not only do you need to help her find a way to organize them, you need to emphasize that she is to take care of the papers. That means all of the papers in her possession must be flat and readable. Eventually, she'll connect that requirement with the absolute necessity to keep her papers in stiff folders that are clearly labeled by subject or task (e.g., "Math" or "Papers to Be Signed").

Early in the school year, encourage your child to organize her desk, locker, and/or backpack in a way that makes sense to her. There are almost endless variations; the key is that it works for *her*. You might work with her teacher to see that the class has a weekly "housekeeping" day to clean out their desks. If it's an activity for the entire class, she won't feel singled out and she'll have an opportunity to watch how others organize their workspaces. Also, make a weekly project of cleaning out her backpack. Try to make it fun, or at least share the misery—you clean out your purse or your briefcase at the same time. The idea is to help her see that this is a skill she'll use for the rest of her life.

One issue many parents report relates to homework that's done, but that their child forgets to turn in. This might be a memory issue, a focus issue, or an organizational issue. If you think this happens simply because your child is disorganized, make her homework folder stand out in some major way. Also, in her daily planner (and we strongly encourage you to teach her how to use one), she needs to write a reminder not just to do the homework, but on the day that it's due, to hand it in. Get her into the mindset that homework isn't finished until it's been delivered to the proper place.

On the other side of the coin, your child will become really frustrated if she's discarded papers and study guides that she'll later need for test review. We recommend keeping a file cabinet or file box at home, so she can keep important papers. Not only will this help her academically, but every time she sorts through and decides what to keep and what to file, she's also getting practice in organizational skills.

In the Community

Because organizing your belongings is such a personal thing, it doesn't always affect others directly. But there are a number of indirect effects of disorganization, such as the following:

- A child fails to bring all of the required sports equipment to his soccer match and can't play. This disappoints the rest of the team and may influence the outcome of the game.

- A child is part of a group effort, and because his portion of it is disorganized, the group itself isn't as effective. Let's say that as part of a service project, your child and his friends decide to make sandwiches for a homeless shelter. Everyone is assigned to bring something, but your child fails to organize his contribution. He brings the mustard and the whole-grain bread, but leaves the rye bread at home. The group can only make half the number of sandwiches.

- Time management is a part of disorganization that can make your child late and keep others waiting. This is draining on relationships. Often, children with executive functioning difficulties fail to consider that it takes a certain amount of time to pack up, and it takes additional time to get to events. They truly think that it takes no time at all to transition from place to place and need a lot of guidance in this area.

Suggestions for Teachers

Deficits in executive functioning, like being disorganized, can significantly impact children in the classroom. We offer some suggestions that might help improve classroom functioning.

o When possible, allow students with organizational challenges to keep a second set of books at home.

o Prepare a lesson or lesson series on organization. Teach students what an organized desk, backpack, and locker might look like. Explain why your classroom is arranged the way it is. Show them your own planner and explain how you use it to stay on track.

o Make sure students clearly label everything with a great deal of information—not only their first and last names, but the name of their school, their grade, and your name. If things get lost, they are likelier to be returned.

o Most classrooms have a very structured beginning-of-the-day routine. We suggest you incorporate an equally structured end-of-the-day routine as well. Leave plenty of time for students to organize their take-home belongings, as well as their personal areas. Allow them to sharpen pencils, replenish their paper supplies, or whatever else they'll need to allow them to start strong the following school day.

o Have regular desk- or locker-cleaning days for the entire class, not just for the students who seem disorganized. It helps to look around and see how their friends manage their possessions, because there's more than one way to be organized. You might consider having the children work in pairs or groups; this may help the weaker child process why certain things are kept, why others are discarded, and how to manage his belongings.

Suggestions for Teachers, continued

---

o If a child is particularly scattered or constantly loses his work, books, or supplies, consider having a separate shelf or area just for him. His belongings are less likely to become a huge jumble if they are on view; just make the location somewhat discreet so as not to attract unwanted negative attention from his classmates.

o Remember, organization is tied directly to problem-solving skills. When a child raises her hand and says, "I don't have any more notebook paper," it's not your problem to solve. It's your opportunity to teach a mini-lesson. Your response (time permitting) could be "Where do we keep the notebook paper (if notebook paper is available in the classroom)? Why did we decide to put it there? What would be a better question to ask? How about, 'May I go to the cupboard and get some more notebook paper?'"

When your child's disorganization affects an entire group or team, it's time to step in. We love the idea of making checklists. Pilots never take off without consulting checklists for each and every system on the aircraft. They don't commit the tasks on the checklist to memory, because that could result in an error or omission. Share this with your child as you're introducing the idea of the checklist. You can apply it to all areas of his life—home, school, and extracurricular activities.

Helping Younger Children

Little ones need clear, step-by-step reminders of each task, in order. If we're packing up to go to soccer, make a photo chart of everything the child needs. In this case, your chart would include pictures of all of the uniform pieces and everything that needs to go with him to the game. If you laminate it with clear plastic, he can use a crayon to check off each item as he places it on his body or in his bag and then puts the bag in the car. When you come home, have him use the same checklist to put away his gear, rubbing out each crayon mark as he does so.

Helping Older Children

Although 8- to 12-year-olds can take more responsibility for their own possessions, it's likely they will still benefit from some kind of checklist. You might keep a loose-leaf binder to add the lists he needs, and remove the ones that aren't relevant at the moment. It's helpful if you have older children actually create their own checklists, either on the computer or by hand. It's a great habit that will serve them well as they get older and have more responsibilities.

This is also the period when you can start to teach lessons of time management. Ask your child how long he thinks it takes to get his stuff together for a game. Then use your smartphone, stopwatch, or kitchen clock to find out how long it *really* takes. The idea isn't to make him faster; it's to bring awareness to the fact that being organized is really a time-saver. Then guess how long it takes to get to the field. You can make a game of it by having everyone in the family guess. Then the next time he has a game, you can point to the hard numbers and say, "We found out it takes you 13 minutes to dress and gather up your stuff, and another 9 minutes to get to the park. And we found out it took 3 more minutes to find a parking place and walk to the field. So if your coach wants you there at 7 p.m., you need to start getting ready no later than 6:35." Disorganized people tend to be chronically late, so do your best to help him avoid this trap.

Leveraging Technology

A lot of us keep our calendars and to-do lists on our phones or other devices, and that *might* work for your older child. When we're considering helpful technology, though, the area of organization might not be the place to go high-tech. Why? Because it's one more item your child has to keep track of. Disorganized kids lose devices. A lot. Also, the reminders that phones and other devices provide tend to be somewhat fleeting—a ding or a brief text flag. We really find that for organizing, it's valuable for a child to have a physical, paper checklist. The act of making lists is valuable as children learn to organize their possessions effectively.

Still, creating digital checklists and keeping an online planner may be really helpful for your child. Some families use Google Calendar to organize the family schedules and each person's tasks. You can even assign each person a specific color to easily recognize who is doing what and when. Other families use an organizational app such as Cozi. This app also allows families to share schedules and tasks. You won't know until you try.

Next Steps

After reading this chapter, take a minute for the following exercise.

An idea I can put into action is . . .

_____

_____

_____

_____

_____

_____

_____

_____

_____

_____

_____

_____

_____

_____

_____

_____

_____

_____

_____

_____

_____

_____

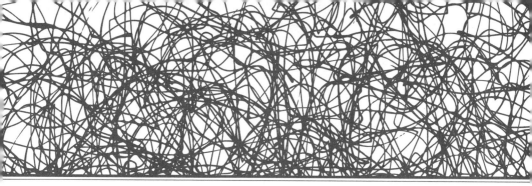

CHAPTER 8
Managing Time

"The journey of a thousand miles begins with one step."—Lao Tzu

Self-Reflection Survey

1. Time management has and always will be problematic in our home.
   a. true   b. false

2. My child has time management skills but does not independently apply those skills.
   a. true   b. false

3. My child's time management difficulties appear mostly:
   a. at home   c. during extracurricular activities.
   b. at school   d. all of the above

4. My child's teacher tries different approaches to help teach my child time management skills.
   a. true   c. I don't know
   b. false

5. We currently use technology tools to help us with time management.

   a. true   b. false

Is It a Time Management Issue?

How do you know if your child has difficulty with time management? If the behaviors listed below describe your child, then you are in the right area.

o Responds slowly to requests
o Waits until the last minute to put on shoes before school
o Does not shower the night before
o Does not place materials in the backpack the night before
o Will not start a project until the day before it is due or until you do it with him or her
o Does not study for a test until the night before
o Waits to complete a study guide or flashcards until the night before a test and then doesn't have time to study
o Does not pack clothes for a vacation until nagged or at the last minute
o Is the last one to clean up and put materials away at school
o Is unaware of assignment due dates

If your child's executive functioning difficulties manifest as difficulty with time management, consider the strategies in this chapter to help at home, in school, and in the community.

What Is Time Management?

Time management refers to how your child uses the hours in the day to accomplish his or her tasks. When it comes to time, we all start on a level playing field of having 24 hours in a day. It's how each of us manages our 24 hours that sets us apart. Productive individuals learn to manage their time because if they don't, time slips away.

Table 6. Guidelines for Time Management Development

3–5 years	■ Very limited concept of time; starting to sequence behavior; can often complete one task before starting another activity.
5–6 years	■ Relate time to events, like birthdays, but no understanding of duration of time. ■ Developing sense of time related to entering events on a calendar.
7–8 years	■ Can think ahead and anticipate events; is developing some understanding of how long various activities take.
9–12 years	■ Can monitor time without assistance from adults.

Don't mistake what we are saying—we are not suggesting you schedule every hour of your child's day. We do want you to teach your child the concept of time and help her learn to be aware of how she uses time when playing with friends, on electronics, studying for a test, or working on a school project. In children with executive functioning difficulties, your son or daughter's internal time clock is not yet perfected.

Developmental Context

In order for a child to have a sense of time, he or she must have memory of past events and be able to sequence them. Russell Barkley (1997) proposed that the ability to sequence longer and longer series of events enables a person to anticipate events farther into the future. This ability further refines the individual's sense of time and enables him or her to delay gratification, based on anticipation of events in the future. Review the chart in Table 6 to understand how time management develops in children.

Perhaps you are thinking, "When I was a child, how did I learn time management skills?" You either had a parent or adult who taught you or you developed them on your own through trial and error. You can support your child by teaching him or her the strategies in this chapter.

At Home

When keeping your child on schedule, do you often feel like a broken record by having to repeat the same things over and over? Peg, the mom of a boy with executive functioning difficulty, expressed the sentiment of many when she said, "How long do I have to keep helping him get ready and out the door in the morning? He is certainly old enough and been told enough to know what to do. But when he's left to be ready on his own time to get out the door, it doesn't happen." Peg tried the checklist approach without success. Next, she tried the logical consequences approach and let her son be late to school, but he didn't mind that and this made her late for work. Finally she resorted to what works to motivate many boys—taking away his afterschool video game privileges if he wasn't ready on time. This approach worked, and her son got ready on time.

Helping the 4- to 5-Year-Old Child

What can you do if your child has time management difficulties? In Chapter 2, we recommended to scaffold support as you teach your child to develop his or her own system. For a 4- to 5-year-old child you must scaffold support by providing advance warnings to prepare your child for upcoming changes. Tabitha prepared her daughter by giving verbal warnings. She would say, "Gracie, in 5 minutes we are leaving for school." Then she'd say, "Remember, in 3 minutes we are leaving, so get ready." Finally she'd say, "It's time to clean up and go." This helped Gracie start to shift her thinking, and while she may not have exactly understood how long 3 or 5 minutes was, Gracie understood a change was occurring very soon.

Parents also teach young children time management by helping children understand words that denote time such as today, yesterday, and tomorrow. You can do this informally through your everyday conversations. In addition, many parents purchase a kid's calendar to hang in the child's room or in a conspicuous place within the home. When his children were young, Jim and his family used a magnetic kid's calendar to discuss the day's activities, tomorrow's schedule, and what occurred in the past. This helped his children understand the concept of time.

Additional suggestions for teaching time awareness include:

o   Use visual picture schedules. Use clip art or pictures to create a visual schedule of the day's activities so your child learns to expect different activities.

o   Teach time awareness by teaching your child how to wait. Most children are notorious for immediately requiring their parents' attention as soon as they start talking to a friend or on the phone. If this happens with your child, teach your child to wait and that interrupting, unless it's an emergency, is not using good manners. For example, if you are talking with a friend and your son runs over and tries to interrupt you, place a hand on his head or shoulder to acknowledge he is there and say, "Just a minute." Then return to your conversation and really wrap it up in a minute. Then turn and compliment your son for waiting. You might say, "Thank you for waiting for Mommy to finish talking. You were so helpful. What do you need?" This simple act is teaching your child time management as well as a host of other important life skills.

o   You can also promote learning time management skills by requiring a verbal child to ask for things using nice words. Aurelia required her son to always say please before she would honor his request. When he said, "More juice," she'd wait without saying anything to see if he responded. If he did not respond, she stated, "Say more juice, please." This subtly taught her son about the concept of time and that his needs may not always be immediately met. She scaffolded support, and he gradually became more proficient at asking using his manners. Sometime he'd forget and when this happened, Aurelia asked, "What are you forgetting to say?" This reinforced his ability to wait.

Teaching 6- to 12-Year-Olds to Be Ready on Time

Children with executive functioning difficulty between the ages of 6–12 often have difficulty being ready on time. Here's how we recommend you teach your 6- to 12-year-old how to get ready on time.

First, decide if it's a *can't* or *won't* issue. If it's a *can't* issue because your child does not have the ability or needed skills to get ready on time, then follow the steps below to teach the skill. If your child knows what to do but just won't do it, then skip to the next heading.

1. Plan ahead to allow yourself extra time. The last thing you need is extra stress in your life, so start practicing this on a day where you don't have to be at a place where you'll personally be penalized if you're late. One client started this on Sunday morning to prepare for getting ready for church because if they were late, it was not a big deal.

2. Explain the expectations to your child.

3. If your child is in second grade or above, self-reflection is an important aspect of learning time management skills. Thus, ask your child to estimate, "How long should this task take?" Putting the estimate in writing gives more accountability and you can use a form like the one in Figure 4. Courtney's son, Richard, is 8, and she successfully used this concept to help him learn to estimate time for getting ready in the morning. She and Richard learned they needed at least 20 minutes once he got out of bed to be ready to eat. Their task estimation chart is included in Figure 5.

4. Consider the consequences. What will occur if he or she is not ready? Often logical consequences are the easiest to enforce. Thus, if he does not have his shoes on when it's time to go, he puts them on during the car ride. When she leaves her homework at home because it was not put in the backpack the night before, you don't drop it off at school. She earns the grade her teacher assigns. Often logical consequences are the ones you and I face if we don't manage our time well, and logical consequences teach us life lessons.

5. Explain the consequences. Ask your child to repeat the consequences.

Task	My Predicted Time	My Actual Time

Figure 4. Blank task estimation chart.

Task	My Predicted Time	My Actual Time
Showering and drying off	5 minutes	9 minutes
Brushing teeth	<1 minute	2 minutes
Dressing	<1 minute	2 minutes
Fixing hair	<1 minute	<1 minute
Socks and shoes	1 minute	3 minutes

Figure 5. Richard's task estimation chart.

6. When it's launch time, allow the extra time. Because most people are visual, consider pairing your verbal instructions with a written directions.

Expect difficulty. Expect push back from your child. Expect to feel frustrated yourself. These are all part of the teaching process and keep in mind the behaviors may worsen before they improve. Nevertheless, keep the course and follow the steps. Giving in helps in the short term but hinders in the long term.

Being Ready: A Won't Issue

Suppose you've practiced the above until you are certain your child knows the skill but still won't do it independently. If your child has the skills but won't apply them, then you must use rewards and consequences. A parent of a child without EF difficulty may scoff at rewarding your child to brush his or her teeth, but that parent does not live with a child with executive functioning difficulty. In addition, remember that the reward or consequence is a temporary support. You are rewarding your child until he or she internalizes the willingness to complete the task independently and consistently.

Continuing with the behavior of getting ready for school, let's say your child can shower and dress on time but won't. Therefore, you implement a system of rewards related to his breakfast. If he is dressed, brushed, and packed before breakfast, he earns a preferred breakfast item. For each 3 (or whatever time you set) minutes he is late, he earns a less preferred breakfast. You explain to your child the rewards listed in Figure 6.

Your child may view this as consequences, but you are simply rewarding the preferred behavior. The child must understand he no longer receives a "free pass." If he is choosing not to follow through with a skill he knows how to do, then he doesn't automatically get what used to be a free choice. Most children will begin to make better choices about getting ready. Some resist and eat a protein bar for a few days on the way to school, but this breakfast choice often becomes less and less frequent.

Thinking Aloud

On the spot teaching often works well for parents because it doesn't require advance planning. In keeping with the philosophy of maintaining a teaching mindset with your child, consider a time when you had a time management problem to solve. Instead of keeping your problem-solving thoughts in your head, verbalize them. Jim

On time or early	Your choice of breakfast or even a special breakfast (e.g., waffles)
3 minutes late	Second preferred breakfast choice (cereal)
6 minutes late	Third preferred breakfast choice (bagel or toast with peanut butter)
9 or more minutes late	Protein bar eaten on the way to school

Figure 6. Sample rewards list.

was traveling to the airport with his family and he included them in planning for the best time to leave the house in order to make their flight. They identified the time it departed and then worked backward as they estimated how long each segment would take (e.g., boarding, going through security, checking the bags, walking into the terminal, parking the car). He could have kept his thoughts inside, but used it as a teaching experience as he verbalized how to plan when to leave. How can you apply the think-aloud concept in your life to teach your child?

Instead of keeping your problem-solving thoughts in your head, verbalize them.

Books for Children

Children enjoy being read to and these are books you can read to and with your child to teach time management skills. Follow the framework outlined in previous chapters, which included: (a) read the book ahead of time to make sure it's appropriate; (b) read to or with your child and pause to discuss the book's ideas; (c) discuss how the book's character used the skill or solved a problem; and (d) discuss how the ideas can help in your family or at school. The books below are available online or in major bookstores.

- o *See You Later, Procrastinator!* by Pamela Espeland and Elizabeth Verdick, for ages 8–13
- o *Get Organized Without Losing It* by Janet S. Fox, for ages 8–13
- o *Late for School* by Steve Martin, for ages 5 and up

- ○ *Late for School!* by Stephanie Calmenson, for ages 4 and up
- ○ *Almost Late for School: And More School Poems* by Carol Diggory Shields, for ages 6–8
- ○ *Henry, You're Late Again!* by Mary Evanson Bleckwehl, for ages 4 and up

At School

Children with time management difficulties struggle equally as much in school as they do at home. Mariella is a quiet third-grade student and a diligent worker. However, she works extremely slowly. She is the last to get her backpack put away in the morning, the last to have materials out on her desk, and the last to finish her classwork. When it's time to line up, she is usually the last one because it takes her so long to get her materials put away. Other students become irritated at her because they are ready and she is not. Even when walking in line, she leaves a big gap between her and the next student because she tends to move slowly. She is constantly being told by her teacher to hurry up. She doesn't want to be last and her teacher and parents are concerned her self-esteem may be affected.

Consider your child. Read the examples below of how executive functioning difficulties appear in school. Do any apply to your child?

- ○ Academic homework not completed
- ○ Dawdles when asked to clean up materials
- ○ Has safety patrol problems with showing up to the assigned post on time
- ○ Doesn't finish lunch
- ○ Only partially or never completes art projects
- ○ Loses track of time and goes to opposite end of playground before it's time to line up
- ○ Does not finish writing homework assignments in daily agenda
- ○ Acts confused when rushed to pack up at the end of the day

Stuart is a 7-year-old boy who is a part of his school's chorus club, but he struggles to manage time, as he is always late for everything. He doesn't realize that even though he is young, when you join a club you have to be on time and stay on task. Because he shows up late to everything, his classmates think, "That's just Stuart." Unfortunately during rehearsal practice, he continues to be late, often ignores deadlines to return permission slips, and randomly switches from task to task because he does not understand time management.

These types of behaviors leave teachers and parents wondering, "How can we teach this child time management in a school context?" The good news is that the same principles that you can apply at home also work in the school context.

For the young child, you'll need your child's teacher's help. Rather than trying to explain your ideas during open house or at pick up time, schedule a conference so you have dedicated time to converse with the teacher. Discuss your concerns, listen to the teacher's concerns, and decide on one or two specific skills. Together, create a plan using the steps below.

Steps for Teaching Time Management in School

1. Identify target behavior.
2. Analyze: Where is the breakdown?
3. Is it a "can't" or "won't" concern?
4. Design a simple to use and manageable plan.
5. Implement the plan.
6. Evaluate to see if it's working.

Jim helped Jennifer (a third grader who often was not in her seat and working on her morning task when the bell rang) and her teacher develop a plan based on these steps. He and the teacher outlined the steps below:

1. *Identify target behavior.* Jennifer is not in her seat when the bell rings.
2. *Analyze: Where is the breakdown?* The problem occurs because Jennifer is social and she talks with others after getting materials put away.

3. *Is it a "can't" or "won't" concern?* It was a "won't" issue because she knows what and how to do it, but doesn't do it.

4. *Design the plan.* The teacher talked with Jennifer and helped her recognize the problem. Jennifer agreed to try a new morning routine. The teacher greets the kids at the door each morning, so she agreed to greet and remind Jennifer. Jennifer agreed to go right to her cubby to unpack her backpack.

5. *Implement the plan.* The teacher reinforced Jennifer with verbal praise and a sticker so that when she earns five stickers she gets to be lunchroom helper, one of Jennifer's favorite school jobs. Jennifer also appeared internally motivated because she knew that completing her morning work would help her earn higher grades.

6. *Evaluate to see if it's working.* The plan was used for 2 weeks. At this point, the stickers were faded out because they were difficult to keep track of and Jennifer started to get into her seat before the bell rang.

Some teachers use their own problem-solving approaches to help students with executive functioning difficulties in time management. Marco, a first-grade boy with ADHD, was last to finish his lunch and gather his trash to throw away. His teacher and the class were always waiting on him to line up to leave the cafeteria. The teacher watched him at lunch and recognized that his family sent his sandwich in a plastic container that Marco couldn't open independently. He had to raise his hand and wait until a lunch monitor came over to open it. This prevented him from beginning to eat his lunch because he was very particular and wanted to eat his sandwich first. His teacher communicated with Marco's grandmother, and she agreed to change from the container to a sandwich bag, which Marco easily opened. This resolved the issue of Marco being the last one done.

A sixth grader, Felix, was notorious for not studying in advance of tests. He had a 504 accommodation plan and received 50% extended time on tests, but this didn't help because he didn't see studying as important. His innovative teacher thought about Felix's interests and located a YouTube interview by his favorite musician discussing how he became successful—part of his message was encouraging students to study in school because his fallback plan was college if he didn't make it in the music industry. Even though Felix had repeatedly heard this from his teacher, it resonated when coming from an artist he respected. When Felix started applying himself to his studies, he still remained a C/D student but his attitude was better.

Social Difficulties Related to Time Management

Your child's executive functioning difficulty with managing time may interfere with his or her social relationships. You notice it. Other parents and even some other children will notice that your child appears late and disorganized. Reflect on your child's social interactions with others. Could any of your child's difficulty be related to an underlying executive functioning weakness with time management?

Do other children become frustrated when your child is slow to play a fast game like tag? Does she take such a long time cleaning up the kitchen items after playing that her friend does most of the work? Does he take a friend to the neighborhood playground, but is unaware of when to return home? Young kids are often forgiving, but frequent blunders can cause friendship problems.

If your child's time management weaknesses are causing difficulty with her social relationships, you can help. Because you know your child best, provide scaffolded support in the weaker areas. If you understand your child does not typically fare well when playing with a small group of children, structure play date experiences with one child at a time and for shorter periods of time. When your child and a friend ride their bikes, provide a cell phone or specific directions such as, "Ride once around the block and then come home. Don't go anywhere else."

Remember that self-reflection is an important part of managing time, so if your child and her friend want to have a lemonade sale, ask questions such as, "How long do you think it will take to set up?

Suggestions for Teachers

Deficits in executive functioning, like having difficulty with time management, can significantly impact children in the classroom. We offer some suggestions that might help improve classroom functioning.

o   Giving a second chance.

o   Providing extra time.

o   Asking him or her to repeat the directions.

o   Writing directions down.

o   Using a written contract.

o   Providing rewards.

o   Waiting patiently without speaking.

o   Modeling expectations.

o   Creating special folder or binder.

o   Using a written communication log.

o   Using a visual timer.

o   Using an audible signal such as a recording of beeps.

o   Creating a visual picture schedule.

o   Creating a work plan.

o   Estimating how much time specific parts of an assignment should and actually take to complete.

How long will you stand outside and sell lemonade? What materials or ingredients are needed?" Asking these types of questions helps children reflect on the process of simultaneously planning and managing time.

Self-reflection is an important part of managing time.

Janna's 9-year-old son wanted to have a friend sleep over. Janna knew the other boy was a nice child who generally got along with her son. She also knew from experience that after a couple of hours of playing, her son would get tired of playing and ask to send the boy home. So, rather than saying no to the sleepover, she had the sleepover begin at 8 p.m. so by 10 p.m., it was time to go to sleep. Her son was happy and so was she.

Although it often takes effort and creative energy, providing supports is a proactive way to prevent problems. As one mom put it, "I can deal with it now or deal with it in a much bigger way later. I'll take now."

In the Community

A child's executive functioning difficulty does not occur in a vacuum but rather permeates through life, so your child's difficulties will surface as he or she interacts with others in the community. Some of these difficulties include:

- o   She does not practice her song on the piano and is not ready for the recital.
- o   He is slow to eat cake at a birthday party and the other kids start the next game and exclude him.
- o   In Boy Scouts, he does not plan for building his Pinewood Derby car so he can't finish on time to race.
- o   Your child plans a bake sale with friends but does not buy the needed materials and can't proceed.
- o   At a restaurant, she can't decide what to order, so you become irritated and just order for her.

- o Use Focus at Will, an app that combines science and music to increase productivity.
- o Use Google Calendar for scheduling.
- o Use Cozi.com for scheduling.

Next Steps

After reading this chapter, take a minute for the following exercise.

An idea I can put into action is ...

_____

_____

_____

_____

_____

_____

_____

_____

_____

_____

_____

_____

_____

_____

CHAPTER 9
Taking Action

"If you really want to do something, you'll find a way.
If you don't, you'll find an excuse."—Jim Rohn

Self-Reflection Survey

1. People view my child as:
   a. lazy
   b. uncooperative
   c. unmotivated
   d. perfectionistic

2. When my child fails to do chores I have asked her to do, I see her as being:
   a. defiant
   b. forgetful
   c. incapable
   d. deficient in task initiation skills

3. I believe that task initiation
   a. can be taught
   b. will improve with age
   c. will always interfere with my child's success
   d. two or more of the above

4. My child's concept of time is:
   a. very weak
   b. nonexistent
   c. excellent for things he wants to do

Is It an Initiation or "Getting Started" Problem?

How do you know if your child has difficulty with initiation? If the behaviors listed below describe your child, then you are in the right area.

o   Waits until the last minute to start projects
o   Has great ideas but rarely acts on them
o   Puts off tasks and never starts on them
o   Complains he doesn't know how to do a job when you know he has the skills to do it
o   Tries to get other people to do things for her rather than do for herself
o   Can always jump right on preferred tasks but procrastinates on things she doesn't like
o   Knows what needs to be done but can't seem to do it

What Is Initiation?

As the name implies, initiation is beginning a job or activity—especially important for nonpreferred tasks or things we would rather not do. Good task initiation would be starting a job when it needs to be done with the right tools to complete it. Initiation doesn't act alone but in conjunction with other executive functions, like attention, behavioral regulation, organization, and memory. Many children with

> *As the name implies, initiation is beginning a job or activity—especially important for nonpreferred tasks or things we would rather not do.*

poor task initiation skills also have a very poor concept of time. They always seem to think that they have more time than is available. The Nike slogan of "Just Do It" makes initiation seem like such a simple skill, when actually it is not.

Possible Contributing Factors to Poor Task Initiation

There are so many factors to consider when trying to figure out why a child procrastinates and doesn't get things done without significant prodding. If it is any comfort to you, research indicates there is a neurological component to poor initiation. Barkley (1997) indicated that evidence from PET scans and numerous studies suggest that "frontal lobe underactivity, particularly under reactivity to events" (p. 290) is implicated in problems in activation when studied in children with ADHD. The person may know what to do but can't translate that knowledge into action. It is as if there has been a breakdown in the sending and receiving of commands.

Juanita, a fifth grader diagnosed with bipolar disorder, attends a special education program with a small pupil to teacher ratio. Her teacher, Mrs. Hill, gets so frustrated with Juanita because every day, in all subjects, Juanita just sits when other students begin the designated task after directions. In trying to figure out how to solve this frustrating problem, Mrs. Hill wanted to make sure Juanita remembered the directions, so she asked Juanita what she was supposed to be doing. Juanita could tell Mrs. Hill what the directions were but still needed specific prompts, such as, "Find a clean sheet of paper, put your name on it, get out your math book, turn to page 54, and do the first problem." Once she had very specific, step-by-step directions, she was able to start the task and actually complete most of it. Mrs. Hill knew enough about mental illness and executive functioning problems to know it wasn't just laziness or obstinacy on Juanita's part, but more a case of the neurons not firing at the proper time to deliver the message or the synapses not receiving the message. Mrs. Hill made a visual schedule on a card for each of Juanita's subjects. When it was time for that subject, Mrs. Hill would place the card on Juanita's desk and stand beside the desk for Juanita to begin the first step. If she followed all of the steps on her own, she could earn privileges or incentives like a homework pass, a chance to do a small job for the teacher, a 5-minute break, or a reduced assignment. As the year went on, the routine became more familiar to Juanita and reduced the load on her executive functioning as more tasks became automatic. Mrs. Hill was able to withdraw the support, and Juanita became more independent in starting tasks.

Deficient executive functioning skills are often only one component of poor initiation skills, and as with everything else, there are other contributing factors related to temperament, physical condition, environment, and the nature of the task itself. If your child has difficulty with getting things done, it is important to put on your detective hat and figure out what some contributing factors may be.

Some of the causes could be related to:

o *Lack of skill*: None of us likes to do things we are not good at, so if your child knows in advance he won't be successful, he will be reluctant to start;

o *Being easily overwhelmed by the number of things to do or the complexity of the task*: Some children are completely bamboozled by a large task and don't understand how to break it down into small, manageable pieces;

o *Perfectionistic tendencies*: Being a perfectionist takes a lot of emotional energy. Some children would rather not do a task than face the fact that they cannot do it perfectly;

o *Fear of failure*: Expectations may be so high for a child that she doesn't think she can be successful; these can be related to being a perfectionist but can also come from unrealistic expectations;

o *Self-concept*: If a child sees himself as capable, he may be more likely to take on tasks;

o *Poor concept of time*: Some children don't understand how much time is left before they have to leave an area or before something is due;

o *Distractibility*: Some children have very good intentions, but get sidetracked before they get around to beginning a job;

o *Boredom*: Constant need for stimulation and boredom with mundane tasks;

o *Poor working memory*: He may not hold the task in mind long enough to get the materials together he needs and get started on it;

o *Oppositional, defiant behavior*: These children do not want to do what they are asked;

o *Depression*: Feelings of intense sadness take away a child's energy and motivation;

o *Lack of sleep*: If your child isn't getting proper rest, either because she goes to bed too late or has difficulty falling or staying asleep, she will not be at her best. Lots of research is coming out about the importance of quality sleep;

o *Physical condition*: Anemia and other physical causes can impact a child's motivation;

o *Learned helplessness*: The child does not feel his effort yields results, so he gives up. Martin E.P. Seligman, Ph.D., coined the term, "learned helplessness" to refer to those children who have learned to wait for things to be done for them rather than taking the initiative and doing for themselves (Vail, 1987); and

o *Lack of motivation*: The child may feel there is nothing in the activity that is worth his effort.

Looking at Solutions

Using your knowledge of your child, determine which of these factors are impacting your child's task initiation and try to provide supports to help bridge the gap from being a reluctant participant to a willing worker. If it is lack of skill, of course you will provide instruction. If she is overwhelmed by the complexity of the task, break the job down into small, manageable parts. If it is related to self-concept or the child's concerns about being successful, obviously there is no quick fix. Children who are perfectionists often seem to have that temperament from a very young age. Their expectations for themselves are exceedingly high. Often they don't try things until they know they can be successful. Many of us have seen children who don't say their first words at the expected developmental milestones and then begin talking in sentences or the child who is delayed in taking a first step because he wants to be sure he can do it before trying. For these children and for those with low self-esteem, it will take years of encouragement and opportunities for success to help them build their competence. Seeing mistakes as an important part of the learning process will be vital.

If your child's poor task initiation has to do with his or her faulty sense of time, use calendars and timers to help the concept of time become more real. Time Timer is a clock that shows time remaining on a task in a visual form. If your child is highly distractible, encourage him to try to think only about the job he is doing until it is complete and of course, try to make sure he is operating in a calm, structured environment. If she is easily bored, try to make the task as interesting as possible, but ultimately she will have to learn that all of us have to complete boring jobs at one time or another! For poor working memory, create visuals and supports as reminders.

The last three reasons children may have trouble with task initiation—defiance, depression, and learned helplessness—will likely require professional help from a mental health therapist or behaviorist. If you suspect any of these problems, get help sooner rather than later. These issues are much too involved to discuss within the scope of this book.

Developmental Context

The development of initiative in young children is quite variable. From your own observations of children, you can see that some children are fiercely independent by nature and want to do everything for themselves. Others are very laid back and perfectly happy for family members to do things for them. These are the children who will need

Table 7. Guidelines for Task Initiation Development

2–3 years	■ Begin to realize they have control over actions (Teeter, 1998).
2–6 years	■ Initiative begins to develop (LeFrancois, 1995).
6–12 years	■ May judge their competence based on comparison to peer group; sense of inferiority may develop (Hébert, 2011).

lots of encouragement and opportunities to develop their independence. When children enter school, independence in many daily activities is expected and strongly encouraged. Children's views of themselves and whether or not they can be successful are important factors in how well they will exercise their independence. As they age, children begin to measure their competence based on comparison to their peers. Table 7 includes the developmental guidelines for task initiation.

In the Home

A child's unwillingness to initiate tasks in the home is always one of parents' biggest complaints. Parents have often gotten into the habit of asking their child three or four times to do something before getting compliance. Try not to get into that pattern, because it is very frustrating to you as a parent, and your children perceive it as nagging. If this is the situation at your house, sit down with your child and discuss the frustration of it all and solicit cooperation from your child in trying to follow through the first time he is asked. As a parent, try to time your requests when you are likely to get compliance, not when your child is in the process of achieving a new level on a video game—unless your request is absolutely necessary. It is fine to give children advance warning, but then try to follow through with a consequence if the request is not followed right away. It will be very difficult at first, but keep remembering that you are training your child for independence—task initiation is a very valuable job skill.

Helping the 4- to 5-Year-Old Child

Most young children do not start nonpreferred tasks on their own but depend on prompts. It is rare for a 4-year-old to begin picking up toys without a directive from an adult. However, if we make a job like this part of the daily routine, we will be helping the child develop task-related skills. Picking up toys could be part of the nighttime routine, as are putting on pajamas, brushing teeth, and going to the bathroom. As we all know, lots and lots of prompting and cueing for each step will be required and you possibly even need a visual chart listing the items to be completed. Some children will need an incentive to increase their level of motivation. However, with repeated practice and much patience and encouragement, hopefully it will become more simplified and ultimately something your child can do with only a single prompt. When we make simple tasks part of the child's daily routine, we are actually promoting independence and making essential tasks seem routine. The ultimate goal is that task initiation will be motivated by internal rather than external cues as they age.

In the book, *Smart but Scattered,* Dawson and Guare (2009) stated that

> Giving children developmentally appropriate chores to do is one of the best ways to begin teaching task initiation. Starting in pre-school or kindergarten, this helps teach children that there are times when they have to set aside what they want to do in favor of something that needs to get done even though it may not be fun. (p. 223)

Teaching 6- to 12-Year-Olds to Start on Homework and School Projects

As we have seen in the press, the subject of homework has come under fire from those in the academic field as well as from parents. Complaints range from calling it a punishment for parents and a thorn in parent-child relationships to suggesting homework does little to advance the knowledge of children and takes the joy out of learning. Some schools have banned homework all together and others have set guidelines. According to Vatterott (2014), the National Parent Teacher Association and the National Education Association recommend the 10-minute rule—10 minutes of homework per grade. For example, a first grader would have no more than 10 minutes of homework and a sixth grader would have no more than 60 minutes of homework. Proponents of homework say it reinforces learning and teaches discipline and responsibility, whereas detractors say it causes family stress.

At this point in time, the homework struggle is a reality for many children and parents. Based on his work with parents and children, Jim has observed that most parents would rather walk over hot coals than try to get their child to do homework. Jim and his wife found that getting their son to start and complete his homework was especially tiresome. Employing Grandma's Rule worked for them. "Grandma's Rule means you have to eat your veggies before you can have dessert. In other words, work comes before play" (Forgan & Richey, 2012, p. 117). Jim's son had to start and complete homework before he could play video games.

In *Raising Boys With ADHD: Secrets for Parenting Healthy, Happy Sons* (Forgan & Richey, 2012), the following guidelines for homework were recommended:

- o Establish ground rules and stick to them. For example, turn off the television and loud music, and don't permit your child to receive telephone calls or text messages during study time.
- o Figure out the optimal time for homework in your household. Some children need a break after school and others cannot be corralled after playing outside.
- o Determine how long your son can work without becoming frustrated. Provide frequent activity breaks.
- o Remember that he may have difficulty figuring out where to start and how to approach different tasks. Help him to learn to prioritize tasks so the most difficult and most important ones are done first. Guide him in making a plan and taking

one task at a time. You may need to cut assignments into parts so he doesn't feel overwhelmed.

o Provide help when needed, but do not become so involved that your son is not independent—a very fine and tricky balance.

o Allow him to use the computer or iPad (with teacher permission) for producing written work.

o If homework time produces too much conflict that cannot be resolved, consider the services of a tutor (if you can afford it). (p. 118)

We also advise you make sure you are providing a distraction-free place for homework that is as inviting as you can make it. Try to make sure the tools that will be needed are readily available—eliminating one more reason to postpone the task.

Additionally, consider setting a specific amount of time for homework. As we have noted, some educators suggest 10 minutes per grade as a guideline but the reality is that many schools expect children to spend at least 30 minutes a day reading. Some children are more likely to be forthcoming about exactly what homework they have to do if they know they have to spend a defined amount of time in study. For example, Janessa knew that her schedule included at least 30 minutes per day of homework. If she said she didn't have any homework, then her parents gave her some academic work to do or she read for the entire time. After several weeks of the new routine, she figured she might as well own up to what homework assignments she had and work on them during that 30 minutes because she would be sitting there anyway. Before her parents established that half hour rule, she would gain more playtime by reporting she had no homework.

Homework, Organization and Planning Skills (HOPS) Interventions by Joshua M. Langberg is available through the National Association of School Psychologists at http://www.nasponline.org/publications/booksproducts/N1108.aspx. It is an easy guide for parents on effective homework management, executive functioning skills, and time management techniques.

More Initiation Strategies

None of us want to create children who are dependent on getting a "pay-off" for doing a job, but some children need a carrot dangling in front of them to jump-start their performance. As we have observed time and time again in our practices, some children seem to be internally motivated and energetic, while others depend on rewards and treats and appear lethargic and passive. If you are the parent of the latter type, then it is important to figure out what is motivating to your child. If she is dependent on external motivation, then you will have to start there. Some children require reinforcement on a fixed schedule with short intervals. You may also find you have to change the reinforcement frequently to maintain performance. Many parents allow the child to select what he is working for from a menu of reinforcers, which can include privileges, time with a special adult, choices of activities, or tangible items. After some success, you can vary the reward schedule and only offer rewards periodically. Of course, the goal is to decrease your child's need for tangible rewards and to substitute verbal praise. The ultimate goal will be the transference from external rewards, either tangible or verbal praise, to having the child initiate the task because of internal satisfaction.

Initiating Short-Term Goals and Transitioning to Long-Term Goals

Children, like all of us, are motivated by success. They are often willing to put in hard work when they feel that their efforts yield results. One way to help them see this is to guide them in setting small goals for themselves and make sure they can monitor the results of their efforts. For example, rather than having them work on learning all of their multiplication tables, break the task down, have them work on learning facts for multiplying by 2, and chart their progress daily using a quick flashcard assessment. Once that is mastered, move to multiplying by 3, etc. If their goal in reading is to increase comprehension, they could set a goal of getting a certain number of comprehension questions correct (make sure the goal is within their capability) and then increase the number required for success as skills increase.

Let them monitor their progress on a simple bar graph chart, whereby they would fill in a square for each question that was correct.

Setting goals encourages all of us to be purposeful about our activities. Rather than just letting whatever comes along take up time in our day, we let our actions be guided by what is important to us. If you drive your child to school or eat breakfast with your child, try carving out some time during those activities for goal setting. If your child is not old enough to understand the concept of setting a goal, then you provide guidance. If she is a shy kindergartener, then a good goal may be to start a conversation with one other child. If he is active and rambunctious, then perhaps a good goal for a kindergartener would be to stay in his assigned area. Older children might choose to increase the length of their written compositions or volunteer to answer a question in social studies class. It gives them a sense of purpose and the satisfaction of a job well done if they are successful. If they have not accomplished their goal, they have a chance to regroup and try again tomorrow.

Once children have gotten the concept of setting a single goal, they can more easily see how single goals can be strung together to make long-term goals. Keeping something in mind that they are working toward can help children resist temptation to be thrown off course, make good choices of activities that can help reach the goal, and give them a sense of purpose.

> *Once children have gotten the concept of setting a single goal, they can more easily see how single goals can be strung together to make long-term goals.*

The sense of confidence we all want our children to have can come from setting and reaching goals.

Books for Children

Children enjoy being read to and these are books you can read to and with your child. Follow the framework outlined in previous chapters, which included: (a) read the book ahead of time to make sure it's appropriate; (b) read to or with your child and pause to discuss the book's ideas; (c) discuss how the book's character used the skill or solved a problem; and (d) discuss how the ideas can help in your family or at school.

- ○ *Reaching Your Goals (Life Balance)* by Robin Silverman, for ages 10 and up
- ○ *The 7 Habits of Happy Kids* by Sean Covey, for ages 4–8
- ○ *Stand Up for Yourself and Your Friends: Dealing With Bullies and Bossiness and Finding a Better Way* by Patti Kelley Criswell, for ages 8 and up
- ○ *The Juice Box Bully: Empowering Kids to Stand Up for Others* by Bob Sornson, for ages 4 and up

At School

Consider your child. Read the examples below of how task initiation difficulties appear in school. Do any apply to your child?

- ○ Is looking around the room long after classmates have begun on the assignment
- ○ Wanders around the library rather than choosing a book and checking it out
- ○ Does not select a peer buddy per teacher direction and must be assigned one
- ○ Sits at his desk while other students are following teacher directions to pack up to go home
- ○ Does not stand up for herself when children try to boss her around or bully her

Beginning Tasks Promptly

Children who do not begin assignments on time waste valuable classroom time, both for themselves, fellow students, and the teacher. Understandably, it is frustrating for the teacher who has planned a lesson and is under pressure to get through curriculum in a timely manner. As we have discussed, there can be many reasons why a child doesn't get busy related to emotional or physical health, self-confidence, academic skill level, classroom atmosphere, and relationship with the teacher, to name a few. As a parent, try to do your part by providing a nutritious breakfast, a bedtime schedule that allows for adequate sleep, and the expectation that classroom work will be completed because it is an important part of education.

If your child is not beginning his classroom work, set up a conference with your child and his or her teacher to brainstorm the issue. If there is a mismatch between the level of the work and your child's skills, can the teacher modify the work in some way? Is there any additional tutoring available at school for your child? If you have the time and patience, can the teacher suggest materials you might use at home to boost your child's skills? If money permits, can you hire a private tutor? Does the teacher feel your child might have a learning disability and qualify for special education instruction? If so, learn how that process starts and proceeds so you can monitor it. Does the teacher feel your child is distracted by watching or talking to others in the classroom? If so, can her seat be moved to a less distracting area? Is the teacher willing to break the task down into smaller units so it might seem less overwhelming for your child? Does the teacher provide positive reinforcement to your child when she does begin work on time? Is a behavior plan needed to encourage task initiation? If so, you could provide incentives at home for days when the majority of tasks were begun on time. A behavior plan to encourage task initiation would be an example of scaffolding and shaping the desired behavior. These are only some of the questions you and the teacher might think about in trying to figure out how to get your child to start on tasks when directed.

Beck, a third grader, is always rummaging around in his desk while his classmates are getting started on assignments. When the teacher prompts him to get started on his work, he looks up at her with a blank look on his face that says, "What work?" His teacher knows he means well, but is so frustrated at having to repeat the assignment and give him individualized attention to get him started on work that is actually quite easy for him. She moves his desk closer to hers. She and Beck work out a signal from the teacher that will indicate directions are about to be given for an assignment. When he sees this signal, he needs to have his eyes on the teacher and listen to the directions. With improved attention to the directions, Beck begins starting his work more promptly. To reinforce this improved behavior, Beck sometimes gets to do special jobs for his teacher.

Standing Up for Oneself

Although standing up for oneself is a little outside of what we usually consider to be initiation, it is a very important skill for school-age children in the current climate, where bullying can have a serious impact. Some children, especially those who are introverted or who have poor social skills, may have difficulty confronting bullying or even seeking support from an adult. If you suspect your child may be one who is hesitant, then it is important to have ongoing discussions with her about the school day. Make sure she understands what bullying is and what to do if it occurs. Role-playing situations can be helpful in preparing her how to respond. You may also enjoy reading the books suggested in this chapter with your child, which will help your child see bullying and how it can be handled in a very concrete, visual way.

Social Difficulties Related to Initiation

Children with difficulties with initiation may have difficulties in social situations for several reasons. Sometimes the child holds back and doesn't initiate interactions with peers or doesn't volunteer for activities. His failure to initiate may leave him standing on the sidelines. Other children may become frustrated with the lack of follow through and learn that the child who is poor at initiation can't be counted on to follow through with commitments. Jillian complained to her teacher that no one wanted her on their team at school. When working on group projects, Jillian intends to fulfill her assigned tasks, but never gets around to it. The rest of her team has to struggle to do her job as well as theirs. She feels bad about it, but doesn't seem able to change her behavior. Her teacher suspects Jillian is overwhelmed with the nature of the task and doesn't know where to start. On the next

Suggestions for Teachers

Deficits in executive functioning, like difficulty getting started on tasks, can significantly impact children in the classroom. We offer some suggestions that might help improve classroom functioning.

- o Try to figure out clues as to why the child is not working. Are there physical or emotional factors interfering? Could it be repeated failure? Is he using his failure to participate as a form of power over adults? Can your relationship with him use repair?

- o When possible, make sure the assignment matches the child's skills level. If it is too difficult and he senses failure, then he will be more reluctant to start on it.

- o If the assignment is too hard, then try to provide as much support as possible or let the child work with a more capable peer.

- o Extra support will likely be needed on new concepts and unfamiliar information.

- o Provide as much practice as you can so the new information can be mastered.

- o If possible, provide an example of what the finished product should look like to increase the likelihood that the reluctant child will start more promptly and have a greater chance of success. Students with initiation problems often aren't clear on "how" to start on tasks, making them appear lazy when they are just unsure and "clueless."

- o For multistep projects, break the project down into small manageable units for the child. Some children are overwhelmed with too much information on a page, so they benefit from having the paper cut into segments and being handed small chunks of material at a time.

- o Give the child priority seating so you can easily prompt him to begin and keep working.

Suggestions for Teachers, continued

○ Remember that children with executive function difficulties are more inclined to completely shut down when stressed or anxious. It is almost as if their executive functions "go offline" when overwhelmed. Try to help students feel "safe" in the classroom, where they are encouraged to take risks as part of learning. Help them see that no one is successful all of the time; failure is often part of getting to the next level.

○ If necessary, use a task initiation and completion chart. There are many different types available online. Some break the child's day down into segments, and the teacher indicates in a box whether the child began working and also kept working. Others give the child points for starting work promptly and continuing to work.

○ Arrange alternate work times for the student to complete unfinished work and provide assistance if possible. He may have a long history of avoiding work, so be patient in your efforts to change it.

group assignment, the teacher assigns Jillian to a group and then helps her break the assignment down into small manageable steps. When the group meets again, Jillian is very proud of fulfilling her responsibility. Her teacher continues to help her break her responsibilities down into steps until Jillian starts to be able to do it on her own.

In the Community

Indicators that your child may have difficulties with initiation may also show up in the community in ways such as these:

o   In sports, she has to be prompted by the coach much more frequently than other girls to get moving and follow instructions.

o   In scouts, he doesn't keep up with his class in earning merit badges because he never starts the projects.

o   In music, she doesn't practice so she doesn't know the song for the recital.

o   At camp, he just sits until prompted and assisted in getting the materials needed for a craft project.

o   She often has nothing to do on weekends because she never initiates any activities with other children.

Setting Up Play Dates

How many times have we heard our children complain of boredom on the weekends because they have nothing to do? Many children with problems in initiation put off planning social activities until it is too late and then are left with nothing to do. If this happens to your child, you might try printing out a large monthly calendar. Look at the available weekends and have your child suggest playmates and activities he would like for the upcoming weekends. Then help her set-up the play date and enter it on her calendar. Do this with her weekly, as she will need your input and support with transportation and scheduling with other parents.

Week	Task	Date Started	Date Finished
Week 1	Make up survey		
Week 2	Ask eight boys to take survey		
Week 3	Tally results and plan activities with leader		
Week 4	Invite two new students to meeting for activity		
Week 5	Invite two more students and implement activity 2		
Week 6	Evaluate meeting attendance and activities		

Figure 7. Ernesto's plan.

Leveraging Strengths

Children who are organized are usually very good at initiating tasks because they have developed a sense of time and its importance. They understand the ordering of tasks and how one thing has to be completed before another can be started. Setting short- and long-term goals can easily fit into their hierarchy of thinking.

If your child is good at seeing the "big picture" and problem solving, but poor at actually initiating tasks, help him break down a "big idea" into components on paper so he can visually see the steps needed to reach the end result. Then help him lay out a plan of what is required daily to reach his goal. Ernesto, a fifth grader, was concerned that his Boy Scout troop was losing members. He told his dad that classmates said they quit because it was boring and no fun. If it were a school or church-related activity, Ernesto would have probably quit too, but he really wanted to earn his Eagle rank as his brothers had done. With guidance from his father and his scout leader, he developed a plan to survey boys his age about what activities they would like to do at troop meetings and then implemented some of the activities. Because Ernesto was a procrastinator and a dreamer, his father helped him write down the plan in Figure 7 to try to attract new members.

Leveraging Technology

Technology, especially calendars and reminders, can be invaluable in helping your child with initiating jobs. Apps or software to consider include:

- o Remember the Milk provides easy to-do lists and reminders.
- o Time Timer allows children to see time progress and how much longer is left.
- o EpicWin is a to-do list where the child earns points and rewards to be used to improve an avatar.
- o On an iPhone, Siri has a voice-activated task list that might be used successfully by older children.
- o Outlook can be customized to color code and list tasks according to due dates.

Next Steps

After reading this chapter, take a minute for the following exercise.

An idea I can put into action is . . .

_____

_____

_____

_____

_____

_____

_____

_____

_____

_____

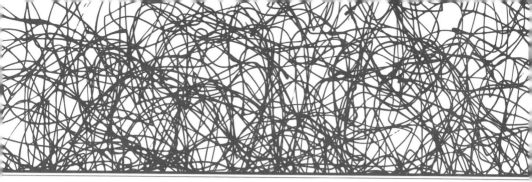

CHAPTER 10

Sustaining Effort

"Life is not easy for any of us. But what of that? We must have perseverance and above all, confidence in ourselves. We must believe that we are gifted for something and that this thing must be attained."—Marie Curie

Self-Reflection Survey

1. How well does your child's achievement match his or her potential?
    a. exceeds my expectations
    b. achieves in accordance with his or her capability
    c. performance falls far below his or her potential
    d. could do better but is generally successful

2. How much prodding is required on your part for your child to stay with a project until he or she has completed it?
   a. constant prodding
   b. occasional reminders
   c. often refuses to even begin a project

3. Motivation:
   a. is always wanting to be the best at everything
   b. is dependent on intellect
   c. can be dependent on the ecological variables, like teacher, interest, health, etc.
   d. can't be cultivated

4. When faced with a challenging task, my child:
   a. gets frustrated but works through it and continues working
   b. quits at the first sign of a challenge
   c. depends on the nature of the task
   d. loves challenges

Answers: 3. c

Is It a Motivation and Task Persistence Problem?

How do you know if your child has difficulty with motivation and task persistence? If the behaviors listed below describe your child, then you are in the right area.

- Has no goals or few interests, despite attempts to provide exposure and encouragement
- Is content to sit and play video games or watch television while peers are active in events
- Is not fazed by poor grades or lack of success in school
- Doesn't seem to care about rewards in school that are appealing to classmates

- Shows general lack of interest in anything
- Starts numerous projects but never finishes them
- Is constantly jumping from one thing to another
- Is fearful of failure and resists any tasks that are even slightly challenging

What Is Motivation and Task Persistence?

Motivation and task persistence involve setting a goal and sticking with the job until it is completed. We can almost think of it as having tunnel vision—keeping our eyes on the end result and not letting distractions get in our way until the task is completed. Motivation is a very complex issue with many facets. We have to consider the temperament and abilities of the child as well as the interplay of environmental factors, like the home and family situation, community, and teacher and peer relationships. Task persistence and motivation are interrelated with other executive functions, including attention, working memory, time management, and self-monitoring.

Motivation and task persistence involve setting a goal and sticking with the job until it is completed. We can almost think of it as having tunnel vision— keeping our eyes on the end result and not letting distractions get in our way until the task is completed.

If your child appears unmotivated, the causes could be varied and a combination of issues related to self-esteem, competence, and skill, in addition to being an executive skill deficit. Children who have experienced repeated failure are generally unmotivated to keep trying, as are children who are subjected to far more negative comments about their performance than positives. It is human nature to avoid things that we know we aren't good at doing. On the other hand, sometimes children are such perfectionists that it is almost painful for them to pursue projects because they are convinced their performance will not meet their expectations. They may appear unmotivated but are instead paralyzed by anxiety and sometimes by depression. Children with ADHD, whether the Hyperactive, Inattentive, or Combined presentation, are notorious for beginning many projects and then flitting from one to another without finishing them. It is important to rule out problems with ADHD, anxiety, depression, and learning disabilities if you perceive that your child is very unmotivated to stick with and finish tasks, especially if there is a family history of any of these disorders. Consult with your child's teacher or pediatrician if you are in doubt. An evaluation by a psychologist or medical doctor could rule out complicating problems.

> *If your child appears unmotivated, the causes could be varied and a combination of issues related to self-esteem, competence, and skill, in addition to being an executive skill deficit.*

Parents report that their children can stick with fun activities for hours, especially playing video games, but have great difficulty completing chores, homework, or activities involving practice to refine a skill, such as in music or sports. That is typical for all of us; we can lose ourselves in activities we find pleasurable, relaxing, or rewarding in some way. Looking at it from a behavioral perspective, something is reinforcing participation in those activities. We continue them because we are getting something out of them—satisfaction of a job well done; pleasure of living in a neat, clean environment; joy of eating food we have prepared; or desire to master a new skill. Children don't come by these appreciations naturally; they have to be taught. It is hard work to constantly monitor children and their household chores because they usually only see those jobs as interfering with their fun. However, it is important to help them see they are contributing to the overall well-being of the family and that all members of the family have to work as a team. Of course, that will be a very hard sell, but it is important for you not to give up because you are building their perseverance, dependability, and work ethic.

Another key to motivating our children is to encourage them to set goals for themselves and to see how sticking with an activity can result in pride and achievement. The work ethic that families want to teach

Table 8. Guidelines for Motivation
and Perseverance Development

Ages 4–5	■ Can stick with some difficult tasks with incentives and adult support
Ages 6–8	■ "Will come back to a task later if interrupted, . . . will work on a project for several hours or over several days" (Dawson & Guare, 2009, p. 267)
Ages 9–10	■ Can stick with a sport or extracurricular activity, ■ Can set short-term goals and monitor progress

their children varies based on family values. It is important to decide what you want to communicate to your child and then make sure you model that behavior in your daily life. If you want your child to stick with a job when it becomes challenging, let him see your refusal to give up on a challenge in your own life.

Developmental Context

Table 8 gives some general developmental guidelines of what to expect at different ages as motivation and perseverance develops.

Perseverance in terms of being able to stay focused on long-term goals is one of the last executive functioning skills to develop. However, even in infancy, parents encourage babies to keep trying to master difficult tasks, like turning over and sitting. Think of all of the laborious tasks your toddler had to master—crawling, walking, and getting food onto a utensil, to name a few. All of these milestones required trial and error, frustration, and tears but resulted in great satisfaction when accomplished. As parents, it is important not to jump in and do things for your children that they are learning to do for themselves. When your child is learning to feed himself, it would be much more efficient—and neater—to grab the spoon and feed him yourself. However, in taking over, you rob him of the confidence that comes from mastering tasks and impede his independence. Being there to encourage him to keep trying to refine a difficult skill is an excellent way to lay the groundwork for motivation and perseverance.

> *Perseverance in terms of being able to stay focused on long-term goals is one of the last executive functioning skills to develop.*

Carol Dweck, a professor at Stanford, has studied motivation for decades. In her book, *Mindset: The New Psychology of Success*, Dweck (2008) discussed her research about how people succeed. She suggests that people either have fixed mindsets where they believe that their intelligence is fixed or a growth mindset where people feel their success is based on hard work. People with a fixed mindset are unwilling to take risks because of their fear that failure will reflect badly on them. Those with the growth mindset see failure as a stepping stone on the path to improvement. She believes people can change their mindsets, but encourages parents to help their children develop a growth mindset from the beginning. She and many other researchers suggest children should be praised for their effort and not their intelligence.

Praise and encouragement are tools to reinforce behavior, but we all know children learn the power of tangible rewards very quickly. If your 4-year-old is trying to learn to cut with scissors, then he will likely persist if he knows a treat or a preferred activity awaits.

In the Home

The most likely place you will see difficulties with sustained effort in the home are in following through on chores. As with most tasks, many executive functions are involved. The child must remember the steps in the process to complete whatever she is doing. For example, if she is doing laundry, she must remember how to sort the clothes, look for spots that must be treated, select the right temperature and type of load, add detergent, and then start the machine. Organization is involved to have the right tools for the job. Of course, the ability to stay focused and avoid distractions is critical, as well as the initiation of the task itself. If things don't go as planned with the task, the child has to be flexible and make sure she is not hijacked by angry emotions and may have to use problem solving to develop an alternate plan.

Completing a chore seems so simple, but when we consider what is involved, we can see many opportunities for the process to break down.

Helping the 4- to 5-Year-Old Child

From a very early age, most young children seem driven to accomplish incredibly difficult physical tasks, like learning to walk. Ideally, we want them to transfer that perseverance to other tasks. Think of the exuberant praise a child receives when he takes his first steps. We don't need to be that exaggerated in our praise for other tasks, but we definitely want to pay attention and praise a child's ability to stick with an activity when the going gets tough. If your child is working on a puzzle or trying to put together a LEGO toy, offer some support when she starts to get frustrated but don't jump in and do it for her. If she can persist and figure it out on her own, that success will be a big boost to her self-esteem and sense of competence.

At an early age, give children simple chores to do that help them see their important role in family life. Start with a simple one-step task that you are sure they can do and gradually add more responsibility. Follow through is important, so make sure the child completes the task and doesn't walk away in the middle of it. Dawson and Guare (2009) suggested chores should be confined to a small area at first, like putting away pajamas. As a child's world expands, he can handle more complex chores that take place in larger spaces, like putting his bicycle in the garage.

Teaching 6- to 12-Year-Olds to Persevere

Anyone who has achieved success can attest to the value of perseverance. Pushing through when you want to quit is an invaluable life lesson, as noted in the old adage, "Quitters never win." As parents, we want our children to learn to set goals and work hard to attain them. It will be much easier to teach your child perseverance if you and he have a good working relationship. Children in this age range try to declare their independence in various ways and to different degrees. One subtle way to assert this independence is not to do what parents expect or ask. Spending the time to become a cohesive team will pay big dividends. You will not lose your authority as the parent, but by giving your child a voice and a stake in the outcome, you will be much more likely to have cooperation. For example, when a skill must be practiced, include your child in goal setting and figuring out the schedule and incentives.

As adults, we know that not everything that has to be done is fulfilling. One sobering fact of growing up is the realization that some unpleasant things just have to be done in order to be a responsible human being. Getting them done and out of the way is often the very best way of approaching these kinds of tasks. Here again, you can serve as a role model for your child as you handle things responsibly just because they need to be done.

Following Through on Skill Practice for Academics or Extracurricular Activities

Trying to get children to practice a skill, like learning to play a musical instrument or refining reading or math skills, is often a very frustrating experience for parents. You know the development of the skill in question is important to your child long term, so why can't you motivate him to work on it? Both initiating tasks and persevering on them are interrelated, as are many executive functions. We refer you back to Chapter 9 (on task initiation or taking action) where we urged you to consider possible reasons your child was reluctant to initiate tasks, including physical, emotional, and temperament issues, as some of those could impact perseverance as well. If you have reviewed and addressed any of these that might be relevant, now it is time to look at the particular skill you are trying to refine.

- o If it is an academic skill like reading or math, then practice at home can really make a difference.
- o Try to help your child see the importance of these skills and how they relate to his success in life.
- o Success is motivating to all of us, so it is important to help your child see that practice will result in improvement. For example, if you are practicing reading, let your child create a card file of each new word he learns. If he has a learning

disability like dyslexia, his progress may be slow, but celebrate each success. Some children enjoy graphing their progress on a simple bar graph.

- o   Help her learn to use her strengths to facilitate her learning. For example, if she is an auditory learner, have her repeat the words she is trying to learn aloud to herself or read them into a tape recorder and play them back while she looks at the word.
- o   Use a behavior plan that rewards him or gives him points if he initiates the practice on his own.
- o   Make sure she has the opportunity to engage in a pleasurable activity following the practice.
- o   Encourage family members to encourage and assist him when possible.

If the skill practice is related to an extracurricular activity, like learning to play an instrument or practice a sport like swimming, it will likely continue to be an uphill battle unless your child wants to participate and sees it as worthy of his time. It may be time to consider the impact the activity is having on your relationship with your child versus the value of the skill. Physical activity is certainly important, and sometimes parents have to allow their child to try many different sports and activities in order to find one that is enjoyable. Our advice to parents is to have your child fulfill his commitment to a team or sport, even though he may want to quit during the season. Even if he feels like he is the worst player on the team, this is an opportunity to teach him the value of commitment and following through with what he said he was going to do. You will be helping him develop perseverance and character.

Following Through on Chores

Most children need some kind of concrete way of monitoring chore completion and incentives to follow through and get things done. Some parents view this as bribing children. Remember you are teaching them skills that they probably really don't want to learn!

Working toward something that is meaningful to them can help the whole process be a little less painful. Incentives don't always have to be monetary or material; they can be choices of activities, special time with a parent or grandparent, or privileges.

It is easy to create your own chore chart using the chart or table feature on your computer or you can put "children's chore charts" in a search engine and come up with many free, downloadable charts, which you can customize with your own chores and incentives. Pinterest is full of creative ways to encourage children to complete chores.

It is always helpful to include children in the planning stages. Let them help pick a chart that will work for them and that is easy for you to monitor. Try to agree on chores to be completed and incentives to be earned. Many children with poor task persistence need rewards or incentives to come very close to the completion of the task. Coming up with a functional plan will include trial and error and revisiting both the plan and the incentives. Rewards don't always have to be tangible. Children might enjoy selecting the menu for dinner on a particular night, selecting a restaurant for a family dinner, or having special time with a family member. Other children are highly motivated by free passes for chores. Some children are easily bored and saturated with a particular system and require changes in the plan itself or the incentives. What works for a while may stop working, so plan on frequent revisions. It will be especially important for you to monitor chore completion and dissemination of incentives when a new plan begins. We know this seems like a great deal of work, but your persistence can pay big dividends well into your child's adult life.

Books for Children

You can use books to help give your child ideas for sustaining effort and these are available online, at libraries, or in bookstores. Follow the framework outlined in previous chapters, which included: (a) read the book ahead of time to make sure it's appropriate; (b) read to or with your child and pause to discuss the book's ideas; (c) discuss how the book's character used the skill or solved a problem; and (d) discuss how the ideas can help in your family or at school.

- *The Energy Bus for Kids: A Story About Staying Positive and Overcoming Challenges* by Jon Gordon, for ages 4–8
- *Be Positive!: A Book About Optimism* (Being the Best Me series) by Cheri J. Meiners, for ages 4–8
- *The Little Engine That Could* by Watty Piper, for ages 3–5
- *Jackson's Plan* (Perseverance Children's Book) by Linda Talley, for ages 4 and up

At School

One of the main complaints teachers have about children is their failure to stick with an academic task until it is finished. When interviewing teachers, we find incomplete work accounts for many low grades. Tasks that require handwriting seem to be the ones that children most often balk at doing. Mary Anne's experience in public schools has shown that children with autism spectrum disorder, learning disabilities, and/or ADHD especially find writing tasks to be very laborious. Many teachers find success with breaking writing assignments down into small manageable chunks so the child isn't overwhelmed with the volume of work. As we have noted previously, many times these children have experienced many failures, so heavy doses of positive reinforcement and encouragement will be required to keep them working. If they can see their effort is producing results, they will be more likely to continue.

Even in optimal conditions, the child who has problems with completing tasks will probably have some days where he is much more productive than others. One thing we know about children with ADHD: They are "consistently inconsistent." Another thing to remember is that change doesn't occur overnight. If he has been unproductive for much of his school life, that behavior is very ingrained and will take time to reprogram. The brain's plasticity allows for change, but when you think about the neurological structure—the billions of neurons, the thousands of connections, and the intricate neurological structure—it is understandable that change will take time, patience, and skill building.

Derek, a fifth grader, came from a family who placed a high value on success. He wanted to do well and always knew what he had to do, but knowing and doing were two different things in his world. He perceived his schoolwork to be mind-numbingly boring. He felt he already knew much of the material. Especially in math, he felt that showing his work was a complete waste of his time even though his failure to do so resulted in low grades. He started to view himself as a loser who just couldn't do what he needed to do. Luckily, he had one teacher, Mr. Bailey, who recognized Derek's frustration and who genuinely liked Derek as a person. This rapport enabled the teacher to work with Derek to establish small goals for himself and then self-monitor those goals. If he began working and continued working on each assignment given in Mr. Bailey's class, he was able to have lunch with Mr. Bailey on Fridays. This opportunity made Derek feel valued, and he enjoyed the exchange of ideas about subjects that really interested him. This incentive and the positive relationship with the teacher were strong enough to enable Derek to overcome the inertia that had stymied his school performance. Even though he still struggled in other classes, he was able to transfer some of that work ethic to other subjects.

For interventions for your child's teacher to use for increasing task completion, refer to the "Suggestions for Teachers" section in Chapter 9: Taking Action. Teacher-initiated interventions for all task-related activities—initiating and continuing to work—are very similar and both require a significant level of oversight by the teacher with gradual transference to self-monitoring.

Social Difficulties Related to Perseverance

A child who does not follow through on responsibilities quickly gains a reputation as someone who cannot be counted on to uphold his end of a bargain. Peers may initially feel "let down" but often quickly move on to other children perceived to be more competent and loyal. Children who have poor ability to sustain effort often have repeated failures and negative experiences, which contribute to a poor self-concept.

Sabrina was always enthusiastic about trying a new sport or activity. However, she quickly lost interest and went on to the next new thing. By flitting from one thing to another, she missed valuable opportunities to make long-term friends and develop competence in specific skills. She made friends easily, but had trouble maintaining those friendships because her interests changed so frequently. When a child like Sabrina continually tries new things, like hobbies or team sports, but never sticks to any of them, other children start to recognize this and begin to think of her as someone who can't be counted on or is a quitter.

Joseph was a gregarious third grader who loved to make children laugh. Children liked to be around him at lunch, but he was one of the last to be picked for group projects in the classroom because children quickly learned that Joseph would not follow through on any assignment he was given. The comments they would make to him lowered his self-esteem and he began to feel like a "loser," as he put it.

In the Community

If your child has difficulty with sticking with tasks until they are completed in the community, he may:

- o   beg and plead with you to be allowed to enroll in a sport and then want to quit after two practices;
- o   insist on getting a guitar and taking lessons and then never want to practice; or
- o   audition for a local theatre production and be selected for a part, but then have to be replaced because he did not learn his lines.

In scouts or community service, children in middle childhood aren't usually given many independent responsibilities because most leaders know that support and directions are needed for follow through because of the children's developmental levels. Children with poor task persistence may set off to do a given task but get distracted and not finish. Tyrell was asked to put the paper plates and utensils at

50 places as his football team prepared for its awards banquet. In the middle of the job, he walked away and started helping with the decorations because they looked interesting. He ended up getting yelled at because the coach counted on him to finish his job. Out of frustration and under the crunch of time, the coach scurried around and finished the job himself. It would have been better for Tyrell to have to complete it, but community leaders often don't have the understanding of executive functioning problems and just want the job done. Children with poor perseverance are generally not considered good community members because they don't hold up their end of a bargain.

Leveraging Strengths

Some older children are very creative and enjoy problem solving. Put that creativity to work by engaging them in how to figure out ways to encourage their own task persistence. Jacqueline, who had a diagnosis of ADHD, Inattentive presentation, always had six or eight projects started at one time. She always felt like a failure because she rarely finished any of them, so people weren't aware of her many skills. She brainstormed with her mother to figure out ways that she could increase her ability to stay with a task until it was completed. She was gifted artistically and wanted to create a portfolio of her work. She set a short-term goal of completing one item a week. If she was successful, she was allowed to purchase one art supply, such as a new brush or shading pencils. When she had 10 items in her portfolio, she and her parents would take a trip to a local art museum. To make her goal easier to reach, Jacqueline decided to minimize the distractions in her environment. She put away extraneous things that might tend to distract her from her goals, used an app to limit her time on social media, and tried to stay more focused and efficient with her schoolwork, which left more time for her art activities.

Other children are very competitive, even with themselves. They might enjoy challenging themselves to see how quickly they could do their chores, while still maintaining quality. They could focus on efficiency and ways to streamline their work. Children who are competitive enjoy success and the feeling of winning. Video gamers love the idea of beating their game, so if you can transfer that competitiveness to wanting success in schoolwork and the desire to master academic tasks and in completing chores, your secrets will be in great demand!

Leveraging Technology

Using a timer can help a student stay on track but requires motivation to use it properly. Clocks, like the Time Timer, provide a visual to show how much time remains in a session and are helpful to encourage young children to stay on task.

Making to-do lists—either by hand or using technology—are a proven way to increase productivity, plus they help foster a sense of accomplishment when things can be checked off the list. They are also an aid to planning and time management because they track how much can be accomplished in a given period. Some of the more popular apps for lists include these:

- o EpicWin is an app where the user creates an avatar who is awarded points for "destroying" chores.
- o iReward Chart allow parents to choose tasks, but children pick the rewards.
- o TaskHammer is an app where the user creates a character, enters "quests" or tasks, and enjoys increasing character status when tasks are completed.
- o Astrid has preset lists of tasks available or you can create your own. It also includes weekly completion dates and occasional compliments. Users can upgrade to provide reminders in the form of voice backup for a fee.
- o Todoist breaks down tasks into component parts. Users can pay more for tasks to be added to a calendar.
- o Remember the Milk includes reminders and prioritizes important jobs.

Next Steps

After reading this chapter, take a minute for the following exercise.

An idea I can put into action is . . .

_____

_____

_____

_____

_____

_____

_____

_____

_____

_____

_____

_____

_____

_____

_____

_____

_____

_____

CHAPTER 11

Planning, Problem Solving, Goal Setting, and Using Critical Thinking

"The intellect has little to do on the road to discovery. There comes a leap in consciousness, call it intuition or what you will, and the solution comes to you and you don't know how or why."—Albert Einstein

Self-Reflection Survey

1. My family's opinion on goal-setting is:
   a. dependent on the circumstances
   b. nonexistent in our lives
   c. something that informs our daily life and is talked about at least weekly
   d. that it takes more time than it would be worth

2. Problem solving requires:
   a. flexible thinking
   b. situational awareness
   c. focus
   d. all of the above

3. My child's planning abilities:
   a. reflect our family's style
   b. are better in school than at home
   c. require significant structure if they are to happen
   d. could definitely be improved

4. My child's critical thinking is:
   a. adequate
   b. an area of strength
   c. an area that needs some help

5. Our family's vacations are:
   a. planned down to the minute
   b. well-organized with room for flexibility
   c. usually left until the last minute
   d. completely spontaneous

Is This a Problem?

If your child's executive functioning difficulties manifest as difficulty with planning, consider these strategies to help at home, in school, and in the community. How do you know if your child has difficulty with planning? If the behaviors below describe your child, then you are in the right area.

o   Works slowly and without focus
o   Unable to prioritize tasks or assignments
o   Starts a task in the middle
o   Isn't sure how to begin a task, errand, or assignment
o   Jumps from one task to another, without finishing any
o   Understands the subject material, but is unable to apply it to an assignment or project
o   Mixes up due dates on assignments

    o   Seems baffled by complex instructions

    o   Unable to grasp the key elements after reading a passage

What Is Planning?

When we discuss planning, we really mean the organization of thoughts, ideas, and goals. Dawson and Guare (2010) defined this set of executive functions as the ability to "create a roadmap to reach a goal or to complete a task. It also involves being able to make decisions about what's important to focus on and what's not important" (p. 1).

When have you made a plan or set a particular goal? Think about your New Year's resolutions. Weight loss? Exercise? Some people set financial goals. But why set goals at all? When we create goals, it provides a focus. If we know where we're going, then we can formulate a plan of action to get there, using a logical progression of steps. With the goal in mind, we solve problems that crop up in whatever way will move us toward the outcome we desire.

Setting the goal provides the motivation, but there's another component—breaking down the required steps to achieve the goal. It requires a level of self-talk that is often delayed in kids with executive functioning difficulties. They have trouble organizing the information in their heads, and they can't distinguish which pieces of information are important. They may get extremely upset along the way if a problem crops up to interrupt how they envisioned a project or task would go. Because it's upsetting to get derailed, they have a hard time conceiving how to fix the problem. That requires judgment and critical thinking, the ability to project outcomes and consequences and make rational, reasonable choices.

As you help boost your child's planning skills, we want to encourage you to shift your emphasis away from the result or the outcome, and onto the effort. Imagine a child who cannot consistently recall her basic addition, subtraction, and multiplication tables and feels trapped in a swirling vortex of math facts. She's probably not going to make A's in math, nor should it be the goal. What we want her to experience is what happens when she puts forth 100% effort, regardless of the outcome. That is a skill that will serve her very well in life, even if she never becomes a true linear thinker.

As we have mentioned before, psychologist Carol Dweck (2008) has written extensively on what she calls the "growth mindset." She believes we all fall into one of two categories: a fixed, limited, and limiting mindset that presumes we can't change, and a growth mindset that's open to the idea that most anything is possible. She cautioned against the dangerous thought that if you have to work hard at something, you must not be very good at it. People with the growth mindset, Dweck wrote, "may appreciate [gifts and talents], but they admire effort, for no matter what your ability is, effort is what ignites that ability and turns it into accomplishment" (p. 41).

Developmental Context

Clearly, the ability to plan, problem solve, and think critically requires competence in a number of other executive functions: focus, organization, working memory. If your child is experiencing delays in any of those areas, it's reasonable to expect further delays in her ability to plan and problem solve. Remember, the frontal and prefrontal lobes of the brain are still maturing well into the mid-20s, and probably even into the 30s for people with executive functioning difficulties. We understand you might find this discouraging, as it signals that the road ahead is a long one for both you and for your child. Try to consider it in a different light, if you can. There is so much room for growth, and so much time.

To think of it another way, it's simply that your child's planning and goal setting abilities are taking longer to come together. Some babies walk at 9 months, and others are content to keep crawling until they're 2 (or older, if there are more extensive neurological impairments). We don't judge this as a lack of will on the baby's part. We instinctively understand that it's a developmental issue. Have the same grace for your 10-year-old as you did when he was a baby, and help him have the same grace for himself. It's not that he'll *never* learn how to plan or problem solve. It's just that he hasn't learned *yet*. One day he will. It might be tomorrow or it might be 5 years from now. Can you find a way to be OK with either outcome? Can you find a way to help your child accomplish these kinds of tasks? Can you help *him* start to see it?

According to researchers at Harvard University, "Having executive function in the brain is like having an air traffic control system at a busy airport to manage the arrivals and departures of dozens of planes on multiple runways" (Center on the Developing Child at Harvard University, 2011, p. 1). We think this is a particularly apt comparison when it comes to the area of planning. We all live complex lives. The ability to bring order to those lives by arranging our thoughts and actions is crucial, and difficult. We do much of that work internally, which is what you need your child to learn to do, too.

Table 9 includes the developmental guidelines for planning and goal setting. Examples of goals (behaviors) to set at each level include:

Ages 4–5
- o   Put away toys you are playing with.
- o   Use nice hands in school.
- o   Complete 10 minutes of an educational app.
- o   Follow one step directions, such as "Bring me the remote."
- o   Go for 20 minutes without asking to leave.
- o   Wait in line for 5 minutes.

Ages 6–8
- o   Bring your dirty plate to the sink after dinner.
- o   Pick up your room with minimal assistance.
- o   Study and pass the weekly chapter test.
- o   Place dirty clothes in the clothes basket or hamper.
- o   Put away clean clothes.
- o   Complete homework with assistance and place it in the correct folder.
- o   Ask how much an item costs and save for it with parental assistance.
- o   Pack school materials in backpack.
- o   Sit for more than 30 minutes through dinner.

Table 9. Guidelines for Planning and Goal-Setting Development

Ages 4–5	■ Able to set and achieve daily goals. ■ Can organize their thoughts enough to complete tasks that have 2–3 steps.
Ages 6–8	■ Able to set and achieve weekly goals. ■ Can plan simple school projects. ■ Can shift attention between two or more tasks.
Ages 9–12	■ Able to set long-term goals stretching to a month or two. ■ Able to break down complex projects into manageable parts ■ Able to problem solve when faced with a challenge.

Ages 9–12

o Independently complete homework and place it in the correct notebook.

o Independently plan and pick out clothes and dress self.

o Independently brush teeth.

o Pack appropriate snack for school.

o Decide on the amount of money required to buy an item and save until you have enough to purchase it.

o Write a thank-you note to a relative for a gift.

o Study and pass a midterm exam.

In the Home

How can you help your child set goals? First, the goals must be age-appropriate. It's unrealistic to expect your first grader's goal to be a trip to a theme park if he earns straight A's all year. A first grader needs a short-term goal: earning an acceptable grade on this week's chapter test. When you set goals that are too long-term, there's the danger that the child will see the goal as unobtainable. He gives up and thinks, "Why try at all?" Max was a third grader who had difficulty taking grades seriously. So his dad decided to give him the chance to earn his favorite video game. His dad told him that if he earned all A's and only one B on his report card, then he could have the game. Max was so excited and agreed to the deal. But on the first math chapter test, he earned a C+. Max was devastated and cried hysterically at home. His dad tried to reassure him that the grades would be averaged and he could still earn the reward, but Max had EF difficulties with shifting his thinking and couldn't get over it. That night he refused to study for his spelling test and scored a D. Max's dad knew the plan to keep Max motivated was over.

When it comes to setting goals, a popular model is to make sure goals are SMART:

o **S**pecific: Can your child see clearly what he wants to achieve?
o **M**easurable: How will you know your child is making progress toward the goal? When will you know the goal has been reached?
o **A**ttainable: Is there a reasonable plan for achieving the goal and likelihood that your child will get there?
o **R**ealistic: Is the goal "just right" for your child's abilities and resources (not too hard, not too easy)?
o **T**imely: Have you identified a specific time limit so your child keeps the momentum going?

Discuss the value of setting goals. Explain that setting goals will help your child work toward something she really wants or needs. Talk about the things she wants to accomplish—don't decide for her. Let her provide most of the input. You can help guide her through this process by asking targeted questions, such as "What do you think you'd like to learn to do?" or "What would you really like to happen in the next 3 weeks (or 6 months or year)?" Also, don't make your child go it alone. Discuss her progress on a regular basis. Ask if she needs help or if she's stuck on a certain part of her action plan. Brainstorm creative solutions to obstacles.

Let's say your child has a reasonable goal. How does she get there? How does she pull a plan out of the swirl of thoughts in her head? How does she organize her thoughts and actions so she's efficient and can make progress? As you work with her, we want to emphasize a point we feel is key. Because there's a tendency to focus on the end result, it's easy for your child to lose sight of all of her effort along the way. If the outcome isn't what she expected, or she doesn't reach her goal,

It's so important to recognize and encourage her efforts along the way. Celebrate the successful completion of each step in her journey toward a goal. That helps provide the confidence to move on.

she may feel like a failure. That's why it's so important to recognize and encourage her efforts along the way. Celebrate the successful completion of each step in her journey toward a goal. That helps provide the confidence to move on.

Kids with EF difficulty often have good intentions, but bad outcomes. Your child may know he has a project due in 2 weeks and can discuss the needed steps to complete it, but when it's time for the rubber to meet the road, he procrastinates. He makes excuses and tells you he has it under control. You tell him to get started because the project is going to take more time than he thinks and you don't want to be running out to find poster board late Sunday night. The two of you banter back and forth until one of you, probably you, blows his or her top and nobody feels good. Yet, the argument spurs him to reluctantly open his book and complete a section. You think, "We have too many years ahead of us to do this every time there is a new project. What am I going to do?"

Here are some suggestions as you work with your child on planning:

o Create accepting environments where children feel free to express their ideas without fear of being wrong or of not being taken seriously. Make sure the setting is a protective "laboratory" where children know they can experiment and practice problem-solving skills throughout each day.

o Give children opportunities for open-ended play activities in long periods of time. Create opportunities for children to initiate and solve their own problems and plenty of time to test out possible ideas and solutions.

o Provide a variety of problem-solving experiences. Offer games, puzzles, discussions, literature, and projects that children design—a wide range of activities that inspire creative and critical thinking and encourage children to stretch their minds.

    o   Don't engage in the back and forth arguing. State your expectations and consequences and let her know you are there for support, but ultimately she earns the grade.

Planning for Projects

When raising a child with an executive functioning difficulty, we continue to help our kids create their own systems. Your child must learn to estimate the time needed to complete each step of the project. We recommend following these steps and the chart in Figure 8 when teaching your child to create a system for planning for projects.

1. Identify the due date.
2. Break the project into smaller sections or tasks. Write them.
3. Estimate the time requirements for each. Write them.
4. Set due dates for each section. Write them.
5. Set an accountability meeting with the teacher. This is an important area that often gets overlooked.
6. Begin. Cross off each area as completed.

Helping Younger Children at Home

We're big fans of making learning fun for little ones, and there are plenty of ways you can help your youngster learn how to formulate a plan. Here, the object is to help them think through the steps to an outcome, and order them in a logical way to achieve that outcome.

Try the step game. Together with your child, plan a pretend outing. It could be a sleepover at Grandma's or a visit to the White House or Fenway Park. Your list of steps might look something like this:

1. Pick up the telephone.
2. Look up Grandma's phone number on the phone list.
3. Call Grandma and set a date.
4. Write the date on the calendar.
5. Find your suitcase so you can pack.
6. Pick out your favorite jammies.
7. Put the jammies in the suitcase.
8. Pick out your favorite outfit for the next day.
9. Put your outfit in the suitcase.

Assignment Name: _____

Assignment Due Date: _____

Step(s)	Estimated Time to Complete	Date to be Done	How I'll Be Accountable

Figure 8. Project planning chart.

10. Find your favorite cuddle toy.
11. Put your cuddle toy in the suitcase.

And so on. You can make the list as long and silly as you like. Here's the challenge for your child, and your chance to celebrate effort. You're not going to ask him to do all the steps in a row. He does Step One successfully, and you congratulate him. Then he does Step One and Step Two, and he earns your praise. Then he does Step One, Step Two, and Step Three, in order. He's building on his own success, and learning about the logical order of things. He's learning about the planning process. He's learning to problem solve ("My suitcase isn't in the closet. This doesn't mean I can't go. It means I have to look someplace else for my suitcase"). He can try to beat his own record; if he got to Step Seven last time you played, try for Step Eight. Either way, because it's all pretend, it doesn't really matter if he gets it right. If he gets frustrated, stop.

You can also help him by making planning an everyday event at your house. During his playtime, ask what he's doing with his blocks and cars, what he's planning to build, and how he's going to do it. Draw him out, and encourage him to elaborate and develop his plans.

Helping Older Children at Home

Cooking together is an excellent, real-world way to help older children grasp the fundamentals of planning. It requires reading a recipe, gathering the proper tools and ingredients, putting them together in the right order, cooking the food at the correct temperature, and remembering to take it out when it's done. The point isn't to make the perfect cookies. It's to get practice envisioning and executing a plan.

Writing for the National Center for Learning Disabilities, Bonnie Goldsmith (2014) advised,

> As best you can, stay constructive in your attitude toward your child's organizational difficulties. Don't criticize. Refuse to allow yourself to think of your child as lazy, unmotivated or incompetent. Give your

child some positive things to say to herself: *I'll get it done. I've done my best. Good job! This is easier than it was last week.*

As adults with plenty of life experience, there's a tendency to listen to our children's plans and offer better, more efficient alternatives. As much as practically possible, try to resist that temptation. Your child can't work on his own planning ability if you do the thinking for him. Instead, ask open-ended questions about the plans he's formulating, and let him experiment. He might teach himself a better way to accomplish something. He may teach *you* a better way to accomplish something.

Books for Children

The following are children's books that can help you teach your child about planning, setting goals, and developing critical thinking. Follow the framework outlined in previous chapters, which included: (a) read the book ahead of time to make sure it's appropriate; (b) read to or with your child and pause to discuss the book's ideas; (c) discuss how the book's character used the skill or solved a problem; and (d) discuss how the ideas can help in your family or at school.

- o *What Do You Really Want? How to Set a Goal and Go for It! A Guide for Teens* by Beverly K. Bachel, for ages 11 and older
- o *Kids Playing Business: Setting a Goal* by Ron Piscatelli, for elementary ages
- o *Learning to Feel Good and Stay Cool: Emotional Regulation Tools for Kids With AD/HD* by Judith Glasser and Kathleen G. Nadeau, for ages 9–12
- o *Isabelle Lives a Dream* by Peggy Sundberg, for elementary ages
- o *How to Do Homework Without Throwing Up* (Laugh & Learn) by Trevor Romain, for ages 8–13
- o *Jump to the Moon: A Book About Setting Realistic Goals* by Bert Miller, for elementary ages
- o *Go Ahead and Dream* by Karen Kingsbury and Alex Smith, for ages 4–8

At School

More than anywhere else, children learn critical thinking skills in the classroom. You can share the following strategies with your child's teacher and also practice them at home:

- Classification plays an important role in critical thinking because it requires identification and sorting according to rules that kids must discover, understand, and apply. When your child plays classification games, follow up the activity by asking questions about the similarities and differences between the groups. You can sort everything from blocks and LEGOs, to books, to crayons and markers to promote critical thinking.

- In a group setting, students are exposed to the thought processes of their peers. Thus, they can begin to understand how others think and that there are multiple ways of approaching problems—not just one correct way. When possible, give your child the opportunity to work with a group.

- Ask open-ended questions. Asking questions that don't have one right answer encourages children to respond creatively without being afraid of giving the wrong answer.

- When reading a story, ask questions not directly from the story but those that make your child synthesize information from the story, or ask her to create an alternate ending to the story.

Helping Younger Children at School

Structure will always help a child who struggles with planning and execution of a task. Step-by-step photo checklists can be a great help. You can "play school" at home to help familiarize your young child with what's expected of her. Ask her teacher how the children transition from one subject to another, for example, and practice it at home. Let your child pretend *she's* the teacher, and have her devise a lesson plan to teach you.

Helping Older Children at School

We've already discussed the value of using checklists and a planner to help your child with daily homework and long-term projects (Chapter 7). These written reminders help him organize his thoughts as well as the materials he'll need to gather to complete the work. Don't forget to teach your child how to use his planner; he may have no idea.

Time management is an essential part of planning for schoolwork. Children with executive functioning difficulty have a faulty sense of time and underestimate, or don't estimate at all, how long a project will take to complete. Many educational specialists recommend having your child estimate how long different kinds of homework assignments will take to complete. She can estimate how long it will take to prepare flashcards separately from how long she'll need to study the flashcards. He can estimate how long his math will take to complete as compared to a writing assignment. These types of tasks are incremental steps that will help a child estimate how long each step will take when he gets a larger project assignment.

In the Community

Almost everything your child does requires some sort of plan. Ask him to make a list of all the things she enjoys. It could include:

o   sports,
o   sleepovers,
o   going to a restaurant,
o   parties,
o   going to the mall,
o   having a friend over to play,
o   going to visit grandparents, and
o   going to a theme park.

As parents, we tend to be cruise directors for our children's lives. We make the phone calls to arrange the play dates. We buy the friend's birthday present. But when we do that, we're not teaching our kids

Suggestions for Teachers

Deficits in executive functioning, like having difficulty with problem solving, setting goals, and using critical thinking can significantly impact children in the classroom. We offer some suggestions that might help improve classroom functioning.

o For some children, the open-ended nature of some tasks or projects is more than they can process. Rather than assigning your students to write a report on their hero, you might select a handful of heroic figures from which they can choose.

o Students who are challenged in planning often are unable to visualize who they might one day become. Try a goal-setting exercise that allows your students to dream big dreams, and then have them break down those dreams into real, doable steps. One child says she wants to be an astronaut? Great. Have her learn how a person becomes an astronaut in real life.

o Encourage your students to include a planning day at the beginning of every long-term project. Also, discuss the concept of taking "planning breaks" at several stages of the project, such as when she needs to make a list of resources, needs to create an outline, or needs to place pieces of the project together into the final form.

o Many teachers now offer their students the option of making a video, performing a play, or creating an art project as an alternative to a written report. We applaud this, because there are many ways to learn. We do recommend, though, that the student be asked to plan those kinds of projects just as methodically, if only to reinforce his or her skills in planning and prioritizing.

o Allowing your students to work in groups helps them see how their classmates plan and set goals. Challenge your students to work together to plan something fun. Perhaps you could split them into groups, and working with parents or volunteers, each group can plan a holiday party. Or older children can divide into groups to plan a community service project.

how to make and execute the plans that affect not only them, but also their friend, coaches, and family members.

Julia was invited to her friend Lily's eighth birthday party. The weekend before the party, Julia and her dad sat down to make a plan. They made a list of Lily's interests, and Julia suggested several possible gifts based on that list. When they went shopping together, Julia selected Lily's present from among three choices in a certain price range. Later, they wrapped the package together. Julia saw how much planning goes into her attendance at a friend's event, and she made most of the important decisions.

Leveraging Strengths

Students with executive functioning difficulties in planning and critical thinking often are extremely creative. They might have such outrageously complex, imaginative ideas that it's hard for them to know how to get from Point A to Point B. You can show them how to use that creativity by helping your child plan a project, event, or activity in her areas of strength. If your daughter enjoys cooking, work with her to plan a simple meal. When Jim's son was in elementary school, he enjoyed Home Depot kids' workshops, where he followed a plan to create a birdhouse, jewelry box, and sailboat. As an adolescent, Jim's son excelled in Minecraft, so the two of them planned how to build a website filled with Minecraft tips and tricks. This process was a learning experience for both of them and taught Jim's son that good things take time to develop.

Leveraging Technology

Planning schoolwork and long-term projects becomes more challenging the older a child gets. In fact, it's often not until she is faced with the demands of middle school that a child's executive functioning difficulties become apparent. Does her school have a website where homework, tests, and other requirements are posted? Give her the password and have her check the site daily and report back to you.

When writing, your child can use the software Inspiration or Kidspiration to brainstorm ideas. If your child is a visual learner, he can use the software to create a concept map or mind map. Next, the software can create an outline for your child to use as a written plan.

Consider using an electronic calendar such as Google Calendar to plan for each stage of a long-term project. Set notification reminders to keep your child on track.

Next Steps

After reading this chapter, take a minute for the following exercise.

An idea I can put into action is . . .

_____

_____

_____

_____

_____

_____

_____

_____

_____

_____

_____

_____

_____

CHAPTER 12
Children With Two Homes

"Obstacles are those frightful things you see when you take your eyes off the goal."—Henry Ford

Self-Reflection Survey

1. My child's other parent(s) and I are:
   a. friendly
   b. oppositional
   c. neutral
   d. not applicable

2. My child/children have a written calendar or picture schedule to help them understand when they are at Mom's or Dad's house.
   a. yes
   b. no

3. The rules between the two homes are so different that my child/children often use(s) that to pit the adults against each other.
   a. true
   b. false

4. The system we currently use to keep my child's/children's materials organized between the two homes, as well as between the homes and school, is:
   a. highly effective
   b. somewhat effective
   c. not effective
   d. nonexistent

5. My child/children share responsibility for keeping track of possessions and having the right material.
   a. yes
   b. no
   c. it could be better
   d. this is a priority area to work on

Helping Your Child Understand Divorce

No couple enters into marriage thinking they will divorce, but according to the National Survey of Family Growth, 20% of first marriages end in divorce within 5 years. Researchers Wymbs, Pelham, and colleagues reported, "Parents of youths diagnosed with ADHD in childhood were more likely to divorce by the time their children were 8 years of age" (p. 741). You may be one of the many couples who have children during these early years and end up divorcing your spouse. Divorce causes stress and alters your child's view of the world and of relationships. We don't know many families who have experienced divorce without turmoil. If your child already has executive functioning difficulty, then the divorce experience can heighten your child's deficits. One mom described it as, "When he walked out, my life was turned upside down and I could only imagine the long-term effect this would have on the kids. I had to get into a routine for my own sanity and for that of my children."

What can you do to help both your child and your life? After divorce, you can help your child by establishing these three tasks as soon as possible:
   1. A predictable routine.
   2. A visible schedule.
   3. Structure with limits.

If you are wondering why these three items are important, it is because they give your child a sense of stability during a rocky time. Even though you and your ex are living in two different homes, try to establish a consistent routine as much as possible, not only for your child but also for yourself. We have worked with many families who have divorced amicably, and although they are not married anymore, they are cordial, at least when it comes to the child(ren). We hope this applies to you as well, but we recognize that it may not and that you are doing the best you can in the current circumstances. Jim worked with a family where the parents lived in different states and where their divorce was not amicable. One parent e-mailed Jim and wrote:

> Unfortunately his father continues to refuse to speak with me over the phone, so all correspondences are done via e-mail. I have received a lot of negative feedback and it has been both highly discouraging as well as difficult for me to conceptualize. He is very accusatory with his approach with me and has more recently begun to question the way in which I have addressed my son's ADHD. Moreover, he seems very impatient with our son in that he does not seem to realize that our son will have both awesome periods along with some rough ones. He is accusing me of excluding him from information related to my son's ADHD, which is just not the case at all.
>
> My main goals are to continue to support our son with the progress he has made so far (I am so proud of him) and protect him from the contentious dynamic between his father and me. I certainly do not want to exclude his father because I recognize and value his role in our son's life, but at this point I do not know the proper way to go about maintaining his involvement. While I try to respect his concerns because I realize they are very much valid to him and address them as they arise, he has just put up so many chal-

lenges that it just breaks my heart and I have no idea how to proceed.

Jim's advice was to keep the child's interest as a central factor in any communication. This is not always easy to do, but helps everyone in the long run. If you are divorced and can't create an environment that is win-win for the child, then the parent with the highest percentage of custody should try to create an environment with structure and routine. A consistent routine is highly recommended, because it often provides predictability, which allows your child to feel comfortable.

Communicate with your child that rules and expectations may vary between Mom's and Dad's houses, but that the child is expected to follow the house rules at either home. Just make sure both your home and your ex's home have clear rules. Most elementary-age kids are resilient and will adapt to the change, but for those who have difficulty with shifting and being flexible, you'll have to do more preparation.

Books for Children

One way to prepare children for living in two different homes is by using books. Most children readily relate to a book's character and gain understanding. Even if you read the book with your child and he or she does not have much to say at the time, this information was heard and is being processed. You may return to the book's advice at different stages of your child's acceptance of the divorce as his or her needs evolve.

> *One way to prepare children for living in two different homes is by using books.*

Children enjoy being read to and these are books you can read to and with your child to reinforce and teach impulse control skills. Follow the framework of: (a) read the book ahead of time to make sure it's appropriate; (b) read to or with your child and pause to discuss the book's ideas; (c) discuss how the book's character used the skill or solved a problem; and (d) discuss how the ideas can help in your family or at school. Popular children's books about divorce include:

- *Dinosaurs Divorce* by Marc Brown, for ages 3–6
- *Was It the Chocolate Pudding? A Story for Little Kids About Divorce* by Sandra Levins and Bryan Langdo, for ages 4 and up
- *It's Not Your Fault, Koko Bear: A Read-Together Book for Parents and Young Children During Divorce* by Vicki Lansky, for ages 3–7
- *When My Parents Forgot How to Be Friends* (Let's Talk about It!) by Jennifer Moore-Mallinos, for ages 4–7
- *Mom's House, Dad's House for Kids: Feeling at Home in One Home or Two* by Isolina Ricci, for ages 4 and up
- *My Family's Changing* by Pat Thomas, for ages 4 and up

As noted in previous chapters, we recommend a four-stage approach to helping your child. This is especially important to follow in talking about topics like divorce, so we suggest you expand upon this approach in the following ways. In Stage 1, think about your child and what areas may be a struggle. Next, locate one of the above books or your own. Preview the book to ensure it fits within your belief system and that you believe it has the potential to help your child.

During Stage 2, read the book in advance. Think about if you want to read the entire book with your child or just sections. As you read the book yourself, use sticky notes and write down any points that fit your circumstances. Think about how you can use the book's information to help your child with understanding, problem solving, or a strategy to use related to the divorce. You may keep these in the book or stick them to the back cover.

In Stage 3, read the book or sections with your child. After you read the section that you believe addresses your circumstance, pause for a few seconds. Wait to see if your child initiates conversation. If he or she does not, then say something like, "Did you think the character was going to do that? What do you think of how he or she solved the problem?" During this time, you are listening to identify if this solution was one your child already considered or if it was a new idea that needs discussing.

In Stage 4, discuss how the book's ideas relate specifically to your life. Ask your child questions such as, "You know, that sounds a lot like what we are going through. Do you think so?" See what your child says and listen. Don't feel like you need to solve things but simply listen and reassure your child that you understand. After you finish the book, ask your child how what he or she learned could help. Don't talk much but intently listen. Then discuss what you believe could be helpful. Discuss how this can be applied at home or in school and even consider role-playing to practice applying the skill. Conclude by reassuring your child that you are available to talk at any time.

Effects of Divorce on Executive Functioning in the Home

If you are a divorced parent, answer this question, "Does divorce affect your child's home life?" Of course, the answer is, "Yes." You know that on various days and times your child with executive functioning difficulty will struggle with focusing on his or her homework, prioritizing which tasks to complete, or regulating his or her emotions. Your child may retreat to a bedroom or keep a screen in front of her face as an attempt to avoid conversation. Other children act out with anger. In our experiences working with children from divorced families, the primary difficulties seem to be in the areas of planning, routines, pitting parents against each other, and self-regulation of emotions.

Planning

Have you sent your child to his or her other home only to realize a critical item such as an important notebook was not packed, a favorite stuffed animal was left, or a key piece of sports equipment was somehow overlooked? If you're like most busy, divorced parents you spend considerable time looking for forgotten items or driving to drop off items. You've realized it takes more time to plan outings, transitions, lunches, clothes, materials, and packing all of the other items your child will need when living in two homes. If you have executive functioning weaknesses in the area of planning, this creates a double challenge to keep yourself and your child on track. Suggested strategies to help you and your child with planning include:

- o Give yourself more time than you anticipate for completing tasks.
- o Have two written checklists—one for you and another for your child.
- o Create charts.
- o Purchase multiple items so when you forget one you have a second.
- o Create a short list of 911 items with those items you have to double and triple check included (medication, sleeping blanket, etc.).
- o Use technology tools to set reminders for important dates and items.
- o Use a printed calendar to provide your child with a visual schedule of where he or she will be each night.
- o When your child is old enough, include him or her in shared responsibility for planning for life's events.

Routines

As you learned in Chapter 1, your child's executive functioning skills don't fully mature until early adulthood. Therefore, as children, they benefit from the structure you provide. Consistency and routine help children learn to develop their own self-management skills. As different as you and your ex-spouse may be, it is important to try and agree on common procedures and basic routines. If you can't agree, then do your best to maintain consistent routines at your home. Tia has been divorced for 5 years, and her ex-husband still does not give the kids a set bedtime. When they stay at Dad's home, they get to stay up as late as they want as long as they are quiet. Tia believes he does this because it's easier than having to enforce limits. In addition, he wants the kids see him as the "good guy." When the kids return to Tia on Sunday, they grumble about her set bedtime and have difficulty falling asleep Sunday night. Tia has communicated this to the teachers because the kids are always groggy and extremely tired on Monday mornings. Within a day or two, the kids are comfortably back into her routine, but she knows next time they are with their dad, the same thing will happen. Tia has accepted this is just the way it will be and that she'll do her best to maintain structure.

Playing One Parent Against the Other

If you find your child is pitting one parent against another, it is often a child's way of trying to avoid something unpleasant. Some parents view it as manipulative behavior. Regardless of your viewpoint, these actions create stress. You can reduce stress by minimizing your child's ability to play the "good cop, bad cop" game. It is often helpful when the parents temporarily put aside their differences and communicate. You must let your child know the two of you may be living in different homes but you two are still the heads of the households. Many parents find it helpful to meet and discuss their child's behavior with a neutral person such as a coach or counselor. In this meeting, parents can work to try and agree to principles such as these:

1. Decide on a uniform set of rules and then tell the child the rules will be consistent between both houses. In addition, rules can carry over between houses. For example, if the child loses video game privileges at one house, he has also lost them at the other house until he has earned them back.

2. Parents should hold the child accountable and not allow excuses for not following rules. The child must do what is expected or a predetermined consequence is applied. Again, for this to work, both parents have to communicate.

By communicating, even if it's through text messages, parents can minimize the opportunities for the child to pit one parent against another. In the long run, this usually reduces arguing and battling with your child.

Emotional Regulation

Is your child quick to pout, sulk, or get in a funk when things don't go his or her way? When this occurs, your child is showing his or her executive functioning difficulty in the area of self-regulation or shifting. Remember, your child with an executive functioning disorder acts inconsistently and is not always predictable. You may find him to be angry when you make a sarcastic remark one time and laugh with you the next.

Keep in mind that as a parent you should not tolerate disrespect, so if this occurs, quickly respond with a discussion and consequence. Your child can't be allowed to walk all over you. But, when your child is pouting, we recommend you approach the behavior with an honest conversation using these steps:

1. Ask the child how he or she is feeling.
2. Make your face mirror his or hers. Ask your child if your face matches the feeling he or she just stated.
3. Validate the feeling by stating that it is all right to feel things. If appropriate, compliment your child for not acting out with angry or aggressive behaviors.
4. Ask your child if he or she wants to talk about feelings.
5. If the answer is "yes," listen and don't feel like you need to fix or solve things.
6. Respect your child's answer even if it's a "no."
7. Give your child time to rebound and recover on his or her own.
8. Avoid embarrassing your child in front of family or friends.
9. Reassure your child that you are available to listen or talk when he or she is ready.

A key idea to keep in mind is that pouting is a behavior that can be changed. It takes time, repetition, reminders, and practice. Maturity helps. Directly addressing the pouting is usually better than only ignoring it and hoping it goes away. We recommend you discuss it openly with your child, because pouting often is a child's way to say, "I need attention." If it continues or worsens, it may be time to seek outside help from a counselor or therapist.

Effects of Divorce on Executive Functioning in School

Although divorce occurs within a home, it also disrupts your child's school functioning. For a minute, consider yourself at work. Do you find yourself suddenly thinking about the last argument you had with your ex? Do you suddenly well up in tears or recognize your mood changing? Have you ever felt numb? When you first experience divorce, concentrating on simple tasks often takes effort. Your child is experiencing a similar phenomenon in school, and children with executive functioning difficulty often become more scattered and disorganized than they were before the divorce. Make a mental note of this, because you'll observe changes in your child. The good news is that children are resilient and you can help your child with an executive functioning disorder by continuing to provide support with materials and homework.

Materials Management

Sending your child to school prepared with pencils, paper, and proper materials is common sense, but when you or your spouse are in post-divorce survival mode, this is often overlooked. We recognize that during or after a divorce, money is often tight, so it may be hard to purchase additional materials for your child. In addition, if your child frequently changes homes, you are juggling new responsibilities, so checking your child's backpack for pencils is not at the top of your priority list. Yet, when your child is unprepared, it creates unease. That unease leads to doubt and can shake your child's confidence. In contrast, your child has security when prepared with basic materials. It's one less thing your child has to worry about and more things you've accomplished to keep your child on the right track. The following may help you help your child.

- o Promote organization and purchase a pencil box or pouch for your child's materials.
- o Keep extra notebook paper at both homes and in your child's notebook.

- ○ Ask the teacher for an extra textbook to keep at home or learn how to locate them if they are online.
- ○ Ask the teacher to check to see if your child's materials are packed up at the end of the day.
- ○ Ask your child to identify a classmate he or she can call or text if school materials are forgotten or lost.

Homework Help

For a child with executive functioning difficulty, homework is often a nightly battle and divorce intensifies the struggle. You're exhausted at the end of the day and so is your child, so you are not alone if you've wondered, "Was homework invented to torment us?" Homework should only be reviewing previously taught skills, so if your child has not learned what he or she is doing for homework, then arrange a conference with the teacher.

You have enough stress in your life, so try not to battle with your child over homework. You may be thinking, "When was the last time homework wasn't a battle?" We recommend seeking homework help from your child's teacher. You are not looking for a free pass, but short-term relief. Many teachers understand the disruption divorce causes, so if you are open with your circumstances, the teacher may temporarily alter your child's homework. He or she may only require that the most important assignments are completed or accept an excused note from you if homework takes an excessive amount of time.

The following sample letter may help you to request a temporary homework reprieve or adjustment as you and your child become adjusted to the new routine.

> Dear *(insert teacher's name)*,
>
> We are writing to ask for your help and understanding. We are not sure if you are aware, but we have separated and are going through a divorce. This has created a new family dynamic, and we are now living in two different homes. During this process, we may not always complete homework on time. We'll

do our best to get the homework done, but there may be circumstances that make it too difficult. Would you be so kind as to allow homework grace for our child during the next few weeks? Please e-mail or call me to let me know if you can work with us during this difficult time.

Sincerely,

(Insert your names)

This approach has helped many families, so could it work for you? You won't know unless you've tried it.

Next Steps

After reading this chapter, take a minute for the following exercise.

An idea I can put into action is . . .

_____

_____

_____

_____

_____

_____

_____

_____

_____

_____

_____

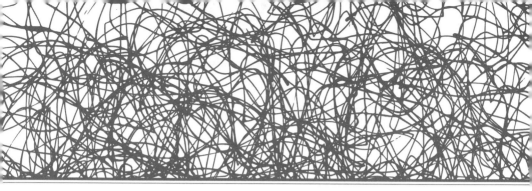

CHAPTER 13
Looking Forward

"Always end the day with a positive thought. No matter how hard things were, tomorrow's a fresh opportunity to make it better."—Unknown

Self-Reflection Survey

1. After reading this book, I think my child has executive functioning problems in the following areas:
   a. keeping information in working memory
   b. shifting, being flexible, and regulating emotions
   c. focusing and monitoring
   d. organizing
   e. managing time
   f. taking action
   g. sustaining effort
   h. planning, setting goals, and using critical thinking

2. In order to help my child with these problems, I:
   a. have a plan in place
   b. need to get more information to develop my plan
   c. still feel like I don't know how to help my child
   d. am going to hire a coach or tutor to help my child
   e. will set up a conference with his teacher to assess his progress and figure out a way to monitor progress

3. After reading this book, I understand executive functioning skills:
   a. are developmental in nature
   b. are functions of the neural circuitry of the brain
   c. can go "offline" when my child is stressed or overwhelmed
   d. can be improved with training and proper interventions
   e. all of the above

Answer: 3. e

Looking Forward

One frequent theme we hear from our clients is concern about their child's future. If you are the parent of children with EF difficulties, then you usually have even more concern, because you see your child's daily struggles to keep materials organized, change classes, write down homework, remember when the next test or assignment is due, and regulate emotions. One parent told us, "How will she make it alone in college? Will I have to go with her?" This mom's concern is heartfelt and valid. Your child may be too comfortable with you filling the role of executive assistant, so it is an uneasy feeling to know that soon your child will be responsible for his or her own living and learning. In this chapter, we offer additional strategies and resources to help you plan for the coming years.

Sure your child may be young now but, looking back on our own experiences, the years go faster than you realize. If you strive to raise an independent and responsible child with executive functioning difficulty into an independent adult, it takes time, effort, and a lot of love. These are how we've approached raising our children with executive functioning difficulty and we hope these principles help you too.

1. Keep the end goal in sight. Some parents get consumed with the daily homework battles, pushing their child to study, and seemingly endless arguing. They lose sight of envisioning the child's future.

2. Empower, but don't enable.

3. Help your child learn to use strengths as well as give her strategies to handle her weaknesses.

4. Coach him in becoming a self-advocate. For example, many teachers appreciate students letting them know how they learn best and what kind of assistance is helpful.

5. Help your child become proficient in using technology to serve as an external assistant to executive functioning skills.

6. Reinforce effort not grades.

7. Keep a teaching perspective. Try not to lecture but instead teach skills. Positively shape and reinforce your child's skill development.

8. Communicate with teachers. The school staff is usually on your side. Most teachers are good-hearted people who want your child to work to his or her potential. If you are really lucky, your child has a dynamo for a teacher. Other teachers are duds. When your child has a dud, rather than engaging in bashing the person, use it as a life skills opportunity and teach your child that life is not always fair. Teach her to stick it out and try to make it the best it can be.

9. Involve others. If you have a spouse, start with him or her. Both of you need to be at teacher conferences, back to school night, and any other important school events. Next, consider creating a relationship with a professional counselor. Once established, schedule time to meet with the counselor on an as needed basis. Both you and your child can benefit from a neutral perspective.

10. Don't quit. Yes, you may feel discouraged; however, quitting on your child is not an option that will make him or her

responsible and independent. Instead take a problem-solving approach. Take each aspect of the problem and together with your child, figure out some possible solutions, implement them, evaluate the results, and go back to the drawing board if necessary.

How to Handle Hurdles

When your child encounters problems, ask yourself the question, "Is this a 'can't' or a 'won't' issue?" By reading this book, you have demonstrated that you are a concerned parent who is very interested in helping your child. However, you don't want your child to become too dependent on you or develop learned helplessness, where she loses the impetus to do things for herself. As her skills develop and mature, you will need to continuously evaluate her skill levels. Gradually remove scaffolds as they are no longer needed, because your ultimate goal is to have her reach independence in as many areas as possible. As we have stressed throughout the book, enlisting your child as a partner in developing and monitoring executive skills is optimal but not always easily achievable.

Incurring consequences for actions, whether natural consequences—like getting a zero—or contrived consequences—like missing TV or computer time—for a missed assignment, is part of growing up. If your child's hurdle is a "won't" issue, she will need a reminder that the presenting behavior is not acceptable. One caveat about natural consequences: Make sure they don't get your child into a hole so deep that she cannot get out and becomes disillusioned. Children with executive functioning difficulty often require a second (or third) chance, so provide a way for your child to make up for times when he messes up.

As you are raising your child, remember the neurological structures that control her executive functions are continuing to develop, so there is light at the end of the tunnel. Be consistent and know that some days will be better than others. Progress rarely happens in a linear way, but usually has its ups and downs.

When you have tried your best and you feel like progress has stymied, consider enlisting outside help. If you live in a metropolitan area, you may be able to solicit the help of a coach for your child's executive functioning difficulties. Coaches usually work with teenagers and adults but also may work with younger children. They can provide support for the parent in setting up structure and helping children and teens set and work toward goals. The coaching sessions are applied, which means kids take action to practice and develop skills rather than simply talking.

In our private practices, we coach students with executive functioning difficulties from around the United States. We support them and their parents in developing interventions and supports that can help their children be more successful. Our coaching is offered in person or using remote video technology and our contact information is on the Internet if you need help. Because most children are accustomed to working with sports coaches, coaching is often more acceptable to children than counseling.

If coaching is not available in your area, see if your child's school has any resources or guidance. Mental health therapists and counselors have experience in working with issues like frustration, depression, and anger. Tutors can assist with remediating academic deficits.

Providing Booster Sessions

Now that you are taking steps to teach your child executive functioning skills, remember that the process is ongoing. It's very common in many areas of the country for women to visit nail salons. Women with acrylic nails require booster sessions every few weeks to fill in the nails. Sports teams train during the off-season and players receive booster sessions. Children receive booster immunizations. As you know, a booster is designed to refresh and maintain.

Let's assume it's the beginning of the school year, and you've taught your child how to establish and follow a morning routine. You teach and support him, and he adequately follows the routine for September. When October comes around, he starts taking longer to get out of bed and get dressed. This throws the morning routine off, so you start to nag and even become angry at your son and barely make it out the door on time. Remember these words: When this happens to you, it is normal. When starting a new routine, all of us usually start out strong and then begin to fade. The same is true for your child. What your child requires is a skill development booster session.

Keep the teaching perspective and have a talk on the weekend when it's not a stressful time. Remember, you don't want to tell your child what to start doing, but guide him to solve the problem using his answers to your questions. Ask questions such as, "Have you noticed getting out the door in the morning has become more stressful? What is happening to make the morning more stressful?" If he does not know, ask, "Are you getting out of bed on time?" Once this fact is established ask, "How can you get back on track so our mornings go smoother and we can leave on time?" Your goal is to empower your child to solve the problem because this creates ownership and independence.

Throughout the book, you've had the opportunity to identify your own action steps at the end of each chapter based on your child's needs and developing executive functioning skills. We've provided a summative tool to help you develop a more comprehensive, longer term plan for your child and ways to enhance her executive skills based on:

o   scaffolding of skills: temporary supports that provide assistance as skills develop;

o   teaching systems of support: longer term supports that may be more or less permanent; and

o   sustaining strengths: identifying strengths to help work around weaker skills.

As parents ourselves and executive functioning coaches, we've experienced that putting plans in writing helps organize thoughts, plan next steps, and guide future behaviors. Consider completing this plan for you and your child.

Step 1. Identify current scaffolding supports in place at home.

I currently help my child using these temporary supports:	Sample
	Use visual timer to help track time for getting ready in the morning.
	Continue to teach and remind to use self-monitoring skills for catching careless errors.
	Oversee weekly chart of chores.
	Continue to provide opportunities for initiation and praise when observed.

Step 2. Identify scaffolding of skills in place at school.

In school, the teacher uses these temporary supports to help my child:	Sample
	The teacher checks the daily agenda to see if I wrote a note.
	At the end of the day, the teacher checks my child's backpack to make sure he has his materials.

Step 3. Identify any additional areas where scaffolding may be necessary in the future at home or at school.

_____

_____

_____

_____

Step 4. Identify systems of support that are in place at home.

At home, we have established these systems:	Sample
	Upon entering, my child always places her backpack in the same location.
	Once home, my child receives a 30-minute break and then we start homework.
	My child sets the table for dinner.
	Our nightly routine is consistent with bath, story, and bed.

Step 5. Identify systems of support that are in place at school.

In school, they have established these systems:	Sample
	A 504 plan is in place based on ADHD diagnosis.
	Upon entering, my child places her homework in the teacher's "in box."
	The teacher has the daily schedule posted and visible.
	My child has preferential seating.
	When my child feels too frustrated, he can go to the guidance counselor's office rather than staying in class and acting out.

Step 6. Identify systems of support that may be necessary in the future.

Looking forward my child may need:

_____

_____

Step 7. Identify your child's strengths and how they can support his or her executive functioning difficulties.

Sample:

My child's strengths include:	Ideas for using these strengths:
Kind heart	*She can be quick to apologize when she has made a mistake.*
Personable, enjoys being with people	*Help him identify friends to call when he has forgotten to bring a homework sheet home.*
Good sense of humor	*Enroll him in extracurricular activities.*
Skilled with technology	*Allow her to use a tablet or smartphone to set reminders.*

My child's strengths include:	Ideas for using these strengths:

Now that you've completed the plan, keep it handy so you can review and refine it as necessary.

We'd like to close by providing encouragement that your child's executive functioning skills will improve. We understand your journey because we've traveled similar paths. We've experienced improvement in our own children, as well as with our clients. We are available to help you experience this, too.

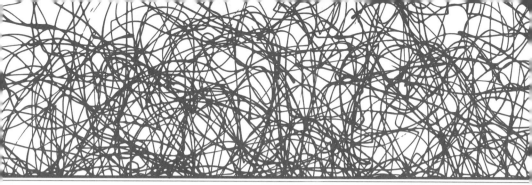

References

All Kinds of Minds. (2014). *Developing saliency determination.* Retrieved from http://www.allkindsofminds.org/attending-to-important-information-developing-saliency-determination

Baddeley, A. D. (1986). *Working memory.* Oxford, England: Oxford University Press.

Baumeister, R. F., Schmeichel, B. J., & Vohs, K. D. (2007). *Self-regulation and the executive function: The self as controlling agent.* In A. W. Kruglanski & E. T. Higgins (Eds), *Social psychology: Handbook of basic principles* (2nd ed., pp. 561–539). New York, NY: Guilford Press.

Barkley, R. A. (1997). *ADHD and the nature of self-control.* New York, NY: Guilford Press.

Barkley, R. A. (2012). *Executive functions—What they are, how they work, and why they evolved.* New York, NY: Guilford Press.

Brown, T. (2005). *Attention deficit disorder: The unfocused mind in children and adults.* New Haven, CT: Yale University Press.

Brown, T. (2006). Executive functions and attention deficit hyperactivity disorder: Implications of two conflicting views. *International Journal of Learning Disabilities, Development, and Education, 53,* 35–46.

Brown, T. (2013). *A new understanding of ADHD in children and adults: Executive function impairments.* New York, NY: Routledge.

Buschbacher, P. (2010). *Making life easier.* Technical Assistance Center on Social Emotional Intervention for Young Children. Retrieved from http://challengingbehavior.fmhi.usf.edu/do/resources/making_life_easie_orgr.html

Campbell, S. B. (1990). *Behavior problems in preschool children: Clinical and developmental issues.* New York, NY: Guilford Press.

Center on the Developing Child at Harvard University. (2011). Building *the brain's "air traffic control" system: How early experiences shape the development of executive function: Working paper No. 11.* Retrieved from http://developingchild.harvard.edu

Chance, P., & Fischman, J. (1987). The magic of childhood. *Psychology Today, 21*, 48–58.

Congos, D. (2006). *9 types of mnemonics for better memory.* Retrieved from http://www.learningassistance.com/2006/january/mnemonics.html

Cooper-Kahn, J., & Dietzel, L. (2008). *Late, lost, and unprepared: A parents' guide to helping children with executive functioning.* Bethesda, MD: Woodbine House.

Dawson, P., & Guare, R. (2009). *Smart but scattered: The revolutionary "executive skills" approach to helping kids reach their potential.* New York, NY: Guilford Press.

Dawson, P., & Guare, R. (2010). *Executive skills in children and adolescents: A practical guide to assessment and intervention, second edition.* New York, NY: Guilford Press.

Diamond, A., Barnett, W., Thomas, J., & Munro, S. (2007). *Preschool program improves cognitive control.* Retrieved from http://www.ncbi.nlm.nih.gov/pmc/articles/PMC2174918/

Dweck, C. (2008). *Mindset: The new psychology of success.* New York, NY: Ballantine Books.

Elliott, R. (2003). *Executive functions and their disorders.* Oxford, England: British Medical Bulletin.

Forgan, J. W., & Richey, M. A. (2012). *Raising boys with ADHD: Secrets for parenting healthy, happy sons.* Waco, TX: Prufrock Press.

Goldsmith, B. (2014). *Executive skills and your child with learning disabilities.* Retrieved from http://www.ncld.org/types-learning-disabilities/executive-function-disorders/ executive-skills-your-child-with-learning-disabilities/

Hébert, T. P. (2011). *Understanding the social and emotional lives of gifted students.* Waco, TX: Prufrock Press.

Kaufman, C. (2010). *Executive function in the classroom: Practical strategies for improving performance and enhancing skills for all students.* Baltimore, MD: Brookes.

Krishnan, K., & Meltzer, L. (2014). *Executive function: Organizing and prioritizing strategies for academic success.* Retrieved from http://www.ncld.org/types-learning-disabilities/executive-function-disorders/executive-functioning-organizing-prioritizing

Kye, C. (2014, June). *Development of lateral prefrontal cortex and executive functioning in both health and disease.* Presented at the National Alliance on Mental Illness Palm Beach County Neuroscience Lecture Series, West Palm Beach, FL.

LeFrancois, G. R. (1995). *An introduction to child development* (8th ed.). Belmont, CA: Wadsworth.

Meltzer, L. (Ed.). (2007). *Executive function in education.* New York, NY: Guilford Press.

Meltzer, L. (2010). *Promoting executive function in the classroom.* New York, NY: Guilford Press.

National Institutes of Mental Health. (2011). *The teen brain: Still under construction.* Retrieved from http://www.nimh.nih.gov/health/publications/the-teen-brain-still-under-construction/index.shtml

Strayhorn, J. M. (2002). Self-control: Toward systematic training programs. *Journal of the American Academy of Child and Adolescent Psychiatry, 41*(1). doi:10.1079/00004583-200201000-00007.

Teeter, P. A. (1998). *Interventions for ADHD: Treatment in developmental context.* New York, NY: Guilford Press.

Tools of the mind. (2014). Retrieved from http://www.toolsofthemind.org/philosophy/glossary/#ef

Vail, P. L. (1987). *Smart kids with school problems: Things to know and ways to help.* New York, NY: New American Library

Vatterott, C. (2014). *Hints to help reduce homework stress.* Retrieved from: http://www.pta.org/content.cfm?ItemNumber=1730

Wellman, H. W., Somerville, S. C., & Haake, R. J. (1979). Development of search procedures in real-life spatial environments. *Developmental Psychology, 15,* 530–542.

Wymbs, B. T., Pelham, W. E., Molina, B. S., Gnagy, J. M., Wilson, T. K., & Greenhouse, J. B. (2008). Rate and predictors of divorce among parents of youth with ADHD. *Journal of Consulting and Clinical Psychology, 76,* 735–744.

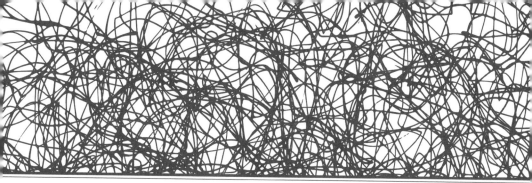

Appendix

The tip sheets in this appendix were developed by the Technical Assistance Center on Social Emotional Intervention for Young Children at the University of South Florida. More resources can be found at http://www.challengingbehavior.org. These sheets were reprinted with permission.

Making Life Easier

By Pamelazita Buschbacher, Ed.D.   Illustrated by Sarah I. Payton

Going to the Doctor/ Dentist

D octor and dentist visits can be very stressful for young children. Routine check-ups can cause anxiety, fear and distress in toddlers and preschoolers. Some common fears for young children include:

- separation from you;

- pain and discomfort;

- stranger anxiety; and

- unfamiliar procedures and people.

The following tips will help ensure that these visits are easier for you and your child.

Tip: Prepare for the doctor/dentist visit.

★ **Schedule smartly.** When you make an appointment for your child, make sure to schedule a time that you believe will work well for him. For example, many children do best early or mid-morning when they are more alert. Avoid skipping naps or meals as this may lessen your child's ability to cope with any negative feelings he might experience.

★ **Choose well.** Choose a doctor/dentist who has experience working with young children and is open to making adjustments based on your child's special needs. Some doctors and dentists specialize in caring for children with developmental disabilities. This is especially important if your child has medical complications, communication and/or behavior challenges. Certain disabilities are at increased risk for dental problems (e.g., Down syndrome and cerebral palsy) and might need more frequent dental visits.

★ **Call ahead** and inform the staff of any special needs that your child might have (e.g., sensory issues, difficulty waiting, sensitive mouth and gums) and of strategies that work for him. Develop a plan with the staff for the actual

1

appointment. Be sure to focus on your child's strengths and strategies for success. You might want to have this conversation in person during a pre-appointment visit (see below).

★ **Pre-appointment visit.** If possible, stop by your doctor/dentist's office before your appointment date. If you are going to bring your child along for the visit, call the office and ask if you can meet the doctor/dentist and take a picture of your child and the doctor/dentist together. During the visit, check out the waiting room. Are there toys/books that your child would enjoy? Are the sights, sounds, or activity levels too stimulating for your child? If so, speak to the staff about other possible arrangements. Take pictures of people and objects in the waiting and/or examination rooms (e.g., fish tank, puzzles, books, the light over chair he will be sitting in, stethoscope, exam table, or other features) and create a personal picture story to read with your child in preparation for the actual visit. Read this to your child several times before the visit. Also, make sure to bring the picture story along to the visit as a reminder of what will happen, what the expected behaviors are, and what choices your child has. When children understand what is going to happen, they are less anxious which can increase cooperation and reduce challenging behavior.

Sample doctor/dentist routines are included with these tip sheets for you to use as a template for your child's personal picture story.

★ **Talk to your child about the appointment in advance.** Consider your child's individual needs and developmental level when deciding when to talk to him about the appointment. While some children may do well knowing a few days in advance, others may do better if told on the morning of the appointment.

★ **Role play the doctor/dentist visit** in advance using a doll or stuffed animal. Allow your child to take a turn at being the doctor, nurse or dentist. Show your child how the doctor/nurse will weigh him, measure his blood pressure, check his ears, nose and mouth. Demonstrate how the dentist or hygienist will look in his mouth, count his teeth and clean them. Do this over and over again so that your child can understand the routine and procedures.

★ **Tell the truth.** Even young children can cope with discomfort or pain more easily if they're forewarned. You child will also learn to trust you if you're honest with him. If your child asks if he will get a shot or need medication, tell him the truth. Let him know what it might feel like and reassure him that you will be there for him. For example, use phrases such as "It will feel like a little pinch (a shot)" and "Daddy will be with you." If you need to leave the room, let him know where you will be.

★ **Share commercial books, television shows or videos** about visiting the doctor or dentist with your child. The pictures can help your child become familiar with what to expect at the visit and with the names of the objects and the people he may see at the office. A sample list of books follows these tip sheets. Your librarian or teacher/interventionist can help you find these as well as other books and videos.

★ **Pack a Waiting Bag.** Waiting in a doctor or dentist's office can be difficult for young children. Many parents find it helpful to take along a bag of favorite things for their child (e.g., books, markers and drawing paper, their personal picture story, doll or action figure, a comfort item or a sticker book). If possible, have your child help pack the bag so he can choose a few of the items himself. Providing choices for your child is a powerful strategy in preventing challenging behavior. You might say, "Do you want to take Mickey Mouse or blankie in your bag?"

2

★ **Read one of the other** *Making Life Easier* **articles, titled, Running Errands**, if getting your child in the car or on the bus for the trip is a challenge.

Tip: Remain calm and positive during the appointment.

Doctor and dentist visits can be stressful even for adults. It is important that your child sees that you are comfortable and confident in his doctor/dentist and staff. If your child becomes distressed during the visit, remember to respond calmly. Ask yourself what the meaning of the behavior is and what might have caused his distress. Once you understand the cause of your child's distress, you can respond with the appropriate strategy.

Tip: Inform staff of strategies that work.

When you interact with the staff of the doctor or dentist office, let them know that you will be using some strategies to encourage your child's cooperation and reduce the likelihood that your child will have behavior challenges. Office staff are usually more than happy to help make the visit go smoothly for the child.

Tip: Use support strategies to decrease the likelihood that behavior challenges will occur.

★ **Use your child's personal picture story.** The personal picture story can be read as you and your child are sitting in the waiting room and during the actual appointment with the doctor/dentist/hygienist as a reminder of what is going to happen next and his expected behaviors and choices. When children understand what is going to happen they are more likely to be calm which can reduce behavior challenges.

★ **Give clear directions.** Give your child a positive direction that assumes he will cooperate. For example, instead of saying "Manuel,

do you want to go see the dentist?" it is better to say, "We are going in the room to see the dentist. Let's go see what interesting things are in his room."

★ **Use "wait time."** A wait time of about 4 to 20 seconds is often all that is needed for a child to process and respond to a request. If your child hesitates, give him the wait time before you give another direction or demand that your child comply.

★ **Provide transition warnings.** Most young children need help transitioning from one activity to another, especially if they are engaged in an activity that is enjoyable. It's difficult for a child to move from an activity he really enjoys to one that he is uncertain of or does not like. To help your child transition, you might:

- Give your child a verbal warning. If he is playing with a puzzle, say "Maleek, I see the nurse. She called your name. I'll help you clean up. Let's go see Dr. Fares."

- Use a visual (picture) warning along with verbal directions. You might show a picture of the doctor/dentist or refer to your child's personal picture book and say, "Cooper, it's time to see Dr. Kind. Let's clean up and go see him."

- Use a countdown or count up strategy and say, "Lei, it's time to see Dr. Ortez. Let's count (pause). 1...2...3...4...5. Okay, let's go see Dr. Ortez."

★ **Provide choices, whenever possible.** Providing limited choices (two or three) for a child in a difficult situation can be a powerful strategy in preventing challenging behavior and redirecting a child to more acceptable behavior and cooperation. Choices help give children a sense of control over their surroundings and activities while still doing what needs to be done! Be sure that ALL the choices you offer are helping reach that goal! For example, if your child has to be examined or take medicine, you might say, "Charlie, let's help Dr. Care. You can sit on the table or sit on my lap. Then he will look in your ears."

★ **Provide frequent and specific praise.** Let your child know when he is being cooperative and helpful by praising him specifically for what he is doing.

3

For example, you might say, "Danny, you played and waited so nicely in the Waiting Room. Let's tell Daddy." "You were so brave. Now the shot is all done. No more shots."

★ **Empathize with your child's feelings.** If your child cries, hits, bites, screams or runs out of the waiting room or examination room, provide a label for how he might be feeling and reassure him. Avoid punishment or threats (e.g., "If you don't sit still, I am going to spank you." and negative, and usually, untrue comments "Big boys don't cry." or "There is nothing to be afraid of." Let your child cry and comfort him by hugging, patting or using a soothing touch.

★ **Follow the appointment with an activity that your child likes** (e.g., a visit to the library or local park). Make sure this is something you can both enjoy together.

★ **Brag about your child's behavior** to a family member or a friend in front of your child.

★ **Encourage your child to share his experience** with another adult such as a parent, grandparent, or friend.

 **Celebrate the little successes along the way.**

In closing, please remember that the team of professionals that support you and your child will have additional specific ideas about how to help your child. Don't forget to ask them! Your child's speech and language therapist, physical therapist, occupational therapist, teacher, or other professionals should be able to help you think about the best way to support your child in their daily routines and community activities. They are usually more than willing to help you make any needed specific supports (for example, a waiting bag, a personal picture story, etc.). If your child is having persistent challenging behavior, you should ask the professionals who work with you to help develop a behavior support plan that will provide more specific strategies to prevent challenging behavior and help your child develop new social and communication skills.

Children's Books to Prepare Your Child for Doctor/Dentist Visits

Your library and bookstore have many books that help children predict and understand what might happen during a doctor or dentist visit. These are some good examples.

Going to the Doctor by Terry Brazelton, MD. Cambridge, MA: Perseus Publishing, 1996.

Going to the Dentist (Mr. Rogers) by Fred Rogers. New York, NY: Putnam Juvenile, 1989.

The Doctor's Office by Gail Saunders-Smith. Mankato, MN: Capstone Publishers, 1998.

Next! Please by Christopher Inns. Berkley, CA: Tricycle Press, 2001.

The Berenstein Bears Go to the Doctor by Stan & Jan Berenstein. New York, NY: Random House, 1981.

I'm Going to the Doctor by Willabel L. Tong. New York, NY: Ladybird Books, a Division of Penguin USA, 1997.

I'm Going to the Dentist by Willabel L. Tong. New York, NY: Ladybird Books, a Division of Penguin USA, 1997.

Going to the Dentist by Fred Rogers. New York, NY: Putnam's Sons, 1989.

Going to the Dentist (Usborne First Experiences) by Anne Civardi, 2010.

Show Me Your Smile!: A Visit to the Dentist (Dora the Explorer). New York, NY: Nickelodeon Publishing, 2013.

Harry and the Dinosaurs say "Raahh!" by Ian Whybrow. New York, NY: Random House Books for Young Readers, 2004.

Technical Assistance Center on Social Emotional Intervention for Young Children
www.challengingbehavior.org

IDEAs that Work

This document is public domain and may be reproduced without permission.
Reproduction of this document is strongly encouraged.
Developed in collaboration with PACER Center (Parent Advocacy Coalition for Educational Rights)

UNIVERSITY OF SOUTH FLORIDA

4

Making Life Easier: **Going to the Doctor/Dentist**

★ **Prepare for the doctor/dentist visit.**

- **Schedule a time** that will work for your child.
- **Choose doctor/dentist** who has experience working with children with special needs.
- **Call ahead** to inform staff of child's special needs.
- **Visit the office** in advance.
- **Role play** the doctor/dentist visit
- Tell your child **what to expect.**
- **Pack a bag of favorite items** to take with you.
- Create a **personal story.**
- **Remain calm and positive** during the appointment.

★ **Inform staff** of helpful strategies.

★ **Use strategies** to decrease likelihood that behavior challenges will occur.

- Give **clear directions.**
- Use **"Wait time."**
- Provide **transition warnings.**
- Provide **limited choices.**
- Provide **frequent and specific praise** for acceptable behavior.
- **Empathize** with your child's feelings.
- Follow the appointment with an **activity your child enjoys.**
- **Encourage your child** to share his experiences.

★ **Celebrate** the successes along the way.

Making Life Easier

By Pamelazita Buschbacher, Ed.D.

Illustrated by Sarah I. Perez

Bedtime and Naptime

Many families find bedtime and naptime to be a challenge for them and their children. It is estimated that 43% of all children and as many as 86% of children with developmental delays experience some type of sleep difficulty. Sleep problems can make infants and young children moody, short tempered and unable to engage well in interactions with others. Sleep problems can also impact learning. When a young child is sleeping, her body is busy developing new brain cells needed for her physical, mental and emotional development. Parents also need to feel rested in order to be nurturing and responsive to their growing and active young children. Here are a few proven tips for making bedtimes and naptimes easier for parents and children.

Tip: Establish Good Sleep Habits

★ **Develop a regular time for going to bed and taking naps, and a regular time to wake up.** Young children require about 10-12 hours of sleep a day (see the box on the last page that provides information on how much sleep a child needs). Sleep can be any combination of naps and night time sleep.

★ **Make sure your child has outside time and physical activity daily,** but not within the hour before naptime or bedtime.

★ **Give your child your undivided and unrushed attention** as you prepare her for bedtime or a nap. This will help to calm her and let her know how important this time is for you and her.

★ **Develop a bedtime and naptime routine.** Help your child be ready for sleep. Babies and young children thrive on predictability and learn from repetition. They like and need to know what is happening next. It

1

is important to establish a routine that both you and your child understand and find calming and relaxing. Bedtime routines usually involve undressing, bathing, dressing in pajamas, brushing teeth, toileting for older toddlers and preschoolers, story and/or prayers (for children developmentally older than six months). The order and content will be different for each family depending on the developmental age of your child, the traditions of your family, and the needs of your child's specific disability.

- Do and say the same things before naps and bedtime. This helps your child transition from active play to sleep.

- Establish a predictable place for sleeping. If you want your child to sleep in his own bed, put him down in his own bed. If you would like your child to nap in her room, guide her to sleep in her room. If you begin the bedtime routine in another location (e.g., the rocking chair) and then move the child when sleeping, your child is likely to wake up during a light sleep cycle and become confused about her surroundings.

★ **Help your child understand the steps in the napping and bedtime routines.**

- First..., then... statements help your child understand and predict what will happen next. You might say, "Sara, it's time to take a nap. First, let's find teddy. Then we can pick a book to read. Then we can climb into bed and cuddle."

- Your child might benefit from a picture schedule or a picture book (photos, clipart, objects) of the steps in her napping or bedtime. This can help her understand the steps and expectations of the routine. It can also help other adults and babysitters put her to bed in a similar manner. Supporting others who put your child to sleep in a way that you have found works will be very reassuring and calming for your child and for them.

★ **Tell your child what might happen when she wakes up.** The day might have been so much fun that your child does not want to take a break for a nap or go to bed for the night. Follow your calming routine, reassuring your child that the fun will continue when she wakes up. You might want to talk with her about what will happen when she wakes. You might want to show her a picture of what is going to happen after she sleeps. For example, you might say, "First, sleep. Then wake up and we go to the park." You might use pictures of sleep and park to help your child understand.

★ **Carry a favorite transition object to bed** (e.g., a teddy bear, a blankie, a book). A transition object becomes another signal to the child that it is time to go to sleep. Some children prefer an object that is soothing to touch or cuddle while resting.

★ **Provide your child with calming, rest-inducing activities, sounds or objects in the routine.** Avoid activities that might excite your child in the hour before bedtime or nap. It is not a time for rough-housing, tickle games, or active play. It is not a time for DVDs or computer games. In fact, you might have an easier time with the naptime/bedtime transition if your child is not engaged in a favorite activity when it is time to start the naptime or bedtime routine. It is important that your routine helps your child prepare for resting and sleeping. Some possible soothing items and activities include sucking a pacifier, hugging a blankie or soft animal, looking through or reading a favorite book, soft music on the CD player, being rocked, a back rub, or singing a lullaby to your child. Reducing the noise and light in the room and nearby rooms is rest-inducing for many young children.

★ **Put your baby or child down for sleep while she is still awake.** Say "good night" and leave the room. By putting your baby/child down before she's asleep, she learns to go to sleep on her own, an important skill for the rest of her life. If she falls asleep routinely in your arms or a rocking device, she might get disoriented or scared when waking up in her crib or bed, rather

2

than cozy and comfortable in your arms. She will not have learned how to put herself back to sleep without your help. When placing your child in her bed, you can provide her with soothing sleep aids such as her security blanket, a stuffed animal, a pacifier, or quiet music.

Tell your child that you will be back to check on her shortly and then be sure to return in a few minutes. She might cry for a few minutes. If so, you can help her settle down again and then leave the room. You can return to her room on regular intervals to offer comfort, but you should not take your child out of bed.

★ **Avoid certain foods and drinks six hours before sleep** (e.g., sodas, chocolate, fatty foods). A little tummy that is digesting sugary, caffeinated or fatty foods can keep a child alert and awake.

★ **Try breast feeding or offering a warm bottle just before bed.** Milk can induce a deep sleep. However, if your child is being potty trained, avoid milk three hours before sleep because it may cause them to have an accident during the night. Remember that a child should never be put to bed with a bottle as that causes serious tooth decay. You want to also remember to help your child brush his teeth after any snack or drink that is given prior to sleeping.

★ **Provide choices whenever possible.** Providing choices for your child has proven to be a powerful strategy in preventing challenging behaviors. Choices you offer at bedtime could be whether the night light stays on or off, what toy the child takes to bed, the story you will read, or if the door is open or shut. This gives your child a feeling of control and helps your child cooperate with your requests. When offering choices, make them concrete and limited (only 2 or 3 choices). For example, you could let your child choose which pajamas to wear (given 2 choices), when to go potty (e.g., before or after brushing teeth), who will give her a bath (e.g., mommy or grandma), or what book to read (given 3 choices), etc.

★ **Reduce noise and distractions in and near her room.** You want to help your child fall asleep by reducing the distractions or things that make her stay awake. For example, if your child would rather stay up and watch television, turn it off until she is asleep. If it is still light outside, consider shades or curtains that darken the room. If adults or other children are talking or playing, consider asking them to move away from the child's room. When an infant or a young child sleeps in a room with the television on or loud conversation happening, she comes to rely on these to fall asleep but doesn't truly get the restful sleep she needs. If it is not possible to keep the environment quiet, consider playing soothing music near the child to block out other sounds (a ticking clock, fish tank, or fan might also work).

★ **Reduce light in the room.** While you want to darken the room, your child might find it reassuring to have a small light on in the room or her bedroom door open slightly and a light on in the hall.

★ **Make sure your child is comfortable.** Check the temperature; what is comfortable for you might be chilly or too warm for your child. Your child might need the security of pajamas that are snug fitting or an extra blanket. She might feel cold even when you think the room is just right. She might need the fan on or off.

3

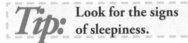

Tip: Consider keeping a sleep diary for a week.

Some children are erratic in their sleep patterns. You might feel at a loss for predicting how much and when she sleeps. A sleep diary is a written log of when your child falls asleep, when your child wakes up, and a calculation of the total amount of sleep for each day. You might also want to write comments about any events that happen that day that could be related to your child's sleep cycles. The sleep diary might help you see relationships between napping and sleeping at night or the consistency of bed- and naptimes. If your child has challenging behavior related to going to bed; you can also write down information that describes the behavior challenges and how you responded. This behavior log could provide you with information about when behavior challenges are likely to occur and what you or others might be doing to rein- force (i.e., pay off) the behaviors. This will help you get a clearer picture of what works and doesn't work in helping your child fall asleep and sleep well.

Tip: Look for the signs of sleepiness.

There are always signs that your child is getting tired. Think about how your child shows you that she is getting tired. Share these observations with others who help put her to sleep. When your child is sleepy, you should assist him in taking a nap or at bedtime. Signs of sleepiness in infants and toddlers might include yawning, difficulty focusing, turning her face away from objects or people, rubbing her eyes or nose or pulling her

ears, falling down or having difficulty pulling to a stand, and losing interest in play. A sleepy baby might arch her back and lean backwards when you hold her. A preschooler might also show the same signs or might have trouble playing with others, complain of a tummy ache, refuse

to follow directions or eat, or become aggressive with others (e.g., pushing, hitting, biting, etc.). Some children become more active when they are tired in an effort to stay awake. Your child might just get "grumpy."

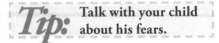

Tip: Talk with your child about his fears.

For a young child, there really are monsters in the room. Your child might tell you he is scared or he might not yet be able to tell you this. See your child's room as a two year old or a four year old does. In the darkness of his room, shadows of toys or furniture might seem frightening. If your child expresses fear, let your child know that you understand his fears (e.g, "you are feeling scared.") and then provide reassurance or comfort (e.g., "That is your toy box making a scary shadow, let me move it so it won't look like a ghost."). Then provide her with a soft toy to hug and other calming activities and/or items suggested earlier. Relock the window, pull down the shade or pull the curtains shut. Check in the closet and under the bed. If your child is afraid of the dark, put a dimmer switch on the light. Start with the light on and gradually dim the light over several weeks. Let your child know that you are nearby and that you will make sure she is safe. Your child might need to know where you will be when she is sleeping, even if you need to use a photo/picture. If you need to remain in the room for your child's safety, keep the light off or dimmed, remain quiet, and avoid interaction.

4

If your child cries or gets out of bed, be supportive and let her know you understand her fears. You might say, "I miss you, too. I'll be in the living room. You'll be fine. We'll have fun in the morning." Calmly return her to bed, make sure that she still has her calming items, reassure her, kiss her good-night, and leave the room.

Tip: Celebrate the little successes along the way!

You might say, "You are getting to be such a big girl, sleeping in your bed with your teddy." Your child's restful sleep makes for a restful you. Then you are both ready for shared days of family fun and learning.

In closing, please remember that the team of professionals that support you and your child will have additional specific ideas about how to help your child. Don't forget to ask them! Your child's speech therapist, physical therapist, teacher, or other professional should be able to help you think about the best way to support your child within daily routines and community activities. If your child is having persistent challenging behavior within this activity, you should ask the professionals who work with you to help develop a behavior support plan that will provide more specific strategies to prevent challenging behavior and help your child develop new social and communication skills.

Is my child getting enough sleep?

Age	Nighttime	Daytime
1 - 3 months	8½ hrs - 10 hours	3 naps (total of 5 - 7 more hours)
6 - 9 months	11 hours	2 naps (total of 3 - 3.5 hours)
12 - 18 months	11¼ hours	1 or 2 naps (total of 2 - 2.5 hours)
2 years	11 hours	1 nap (90 minutes - 2 hours)
3 years	10½ hours	1 nap (90 minutes - 2 hours)

* *Your child will probably transition out of naps between 2-5 years of age.*

Technical Assistance Center on Social Emotional Intervention for Young Children
www.challengingbehavior.org
This document is public domain and may be reproduced without permission.
Reproduction of this document is strongly encouraged.
Developed in collaboration with PACER Center (Parent Advocacy Coalition for Educational Rights)

UNIVERSITY OF
SOUTH FLORIDA

5

Making Life Easier: **Bedtime & Naptime**

* Make sure your child gets plenty of **exercise** during the day.

* Develop **regular times** for bed and naps and stick with them.

* Develop a bedtime and naptime **routine**.
  * Do and say the same things before naps and bedtime.
  * Establish a predictable place for sleeping.
  * Help your child understand the steps in the routines (e.g., use "first, then" statements, picture schedule).
  * Tell your child what might happen when she wakes up.
  * Let your child carry a favorite transition object to bed.
  * Provide your child with calming and rest inducing activities, sounds, or objects in the routine.
  * Put your baby or child down for sleep while she is still awake. Say, "Good night." and leave the room.

* Give your child your undivided and unrushed **attention**.

* **Avoid certain foods** and drinks six hours before sleep (i.e., sodas, chocolate, fatty foods).

* Try **breast feeding** or offering a warm bottle just before bed.

* Provide **choices** whenever possible.

* **Reduce noise**, light, and distractions in and near your child's room.

* Keep a **sleep diary** so you will know what's working (or not).

* **Celebrate** the little successes along the way.

Making Life Easier

By Pamelazita Buschbacher, Ed.D.   Illustrated by Sarah I. Perez

Running Errands

Running errands (e.g., going to the store, bank, etc.) is one of those essential household routines that all families experience. It is often thought of as a "maintenance" activity that is necessary for the family, but not enjoyable for young children. However, there can be huge benefits in taking your young child along. He learns about his community while spending time with someone he loves and trusts, someone who can help him understand the world beyond home and family. Running errands together offers the chance to build self-confidence, curiosity, social skills, self control, communication skills, and sensory exploration. He'll have opportunities to greet and interact with other children and adults with your guidance and support. He will also be able experience the myriad of smells, tastes, sounds, and textures of the greater world within which he lives.

However, running errands can be extremely difficult if the child has challenging behavior. It's not uncommon for families to feel overwhelmed by their child's challenging behavior and resort to only running errands when someone else can care for the child at home. Sometimes, depending on the errand (e.g., a long shopping trip, parent visit to the doctor), that might be the best strategy. Still, there are steps you can take to help you and your child get the most out of these outings.

Tip: Plan for the transition from home to going out.

Let your child know where you both will be going. This can be done verbally, visually (timer, gesture, using sign language) and/or with sound (timer, countdown). Remember to allow time for the transition. Young children need time to shift their focus from one activity to another.

★ **Provide a transition warning.** It is a given that if you have a young child, he is going to have some trouble with transitioning from one activity/place to another.

- You might try giving him a verbal warning and say, "Nashon, we have to go to the store in 5 minutes. When you are done with your puzzle, we can put your shoes on."

1

- Another strategy is to use a timer set for 5 minutes and let your child know that when the bell rings you are both going to get in the car to run a few errands. Remind him as the time gets closer. You might say, "Look, Barry, 2 more minutes then we go to the car." You can use a kitchen timer to help your child or purchase a visual timer that shows the time counting down (your child's teacher or therapist would be able to tell you more about where to purchase a visual timer).

- You might use a countdown or count up and make a game of the transition. You might say, "Okay, I am counting and then we are going to the post office. 10, 9, 8…1. Ready to go."

- You might sing a song to assist him with the transition such as "The Clean-up Song" or "This is the way we put on our socks" (tune of "This is the Way We Wash our Clothes").

★ **Tell your child where you will be going.**

- "First…, then…": You can do this verbally, such as, "Mikey, we are going to run two errands and then we'll be right back to watch a video. First, we are going to the bank. Then we are going to the post office. Then we'll come home and watch your Barney video."

- Some children need a more concrete and visual support of where they are going with you. Many parents have found great success with a travel book. This can be made with a small photo book with blank photo sleeves. To make a travel book, take photos of the places in your community that you frequent such as the bank, health food store, grocery store, post office, grandma's house, the library, the park, etc. Place each picture in a photo page. As you prepare to run your errands, place the photos of the places you will go in sequential order (with home being the final page) for your child. Describe where you will be going using the photos. For example, you might say "First, we are going to the bank, then to Grandma's, etc., then home." You can also use clip-art found on the internet or a picture from a magazine. Always end with home or a preferred destination (e.g., the park, a friend's home). This strategy of planning for a naturally occurring reinforcer as part of your routine works better than bribing your child with an unrelated reward.

- Start with going to just one place and then returning home or to another favorite place of your child's (e.g., McDonald's, the park, etc.).

- Consider planning your trips so that they include a place that your child would like to go.

★ **Provide choices for a transition object whenever possible.**

- Providing choices for your child is a powerful strategy in preventing challenging behavior. This gives him a feeling of control and supports his growing confidence and sense of competency.

- Offering limited choices (2 or 3) versus many prevents your child from engaging in a game where you keep offering different things and your child keeps saying "not that one." You might say, "Michaela, do you want bunny or baby doll to ride in the car with us?"

★ **Prepare a cooler with a snack, a drink and an ice pack.**

- Keep the travel cooler in your kitchen so that it is visible and readily accessible. When filling the cooler, allow your child to decide what snack/drink will go in it. Not only does your child get to make choices, he has the opportunity to help and is more motivated to run the errands with you.

★ **Prepare your diaper bag.**

- It is frustrating for you and your child not to have that needed item when you get somewhere. Keep a list of things that you need in your diaper bag or backpack (some families find that a back-pack is easier to manage and allows you to have two hands free to guide your child). If possible, laminate the list. It'll be more durable that way.

2

As you prepare to leave, read over your list to make sure that you have everything you need before heading out the door. If possible, enlist the help of your child in getting anything that you might need for the bag. If your child needs special supports such as a nebulizer or communication board, those items should be on your list. Additionally, it will help other adults and older children make sure that everything is in the bag.

Tip: Turn getting in the car seat into a game.

Keep in mind that young children love being playful about everything and that from 18 months on up they are interested in doing things independently.

★ **Make getting to the car a game.** (e.g., hop, skip, and follow the leader). Give him a choice of the manner for moving to the car. You might say, "Let's skip to the car" or "Do want to hop or skip?" Or you can make it a race. You might say, "Can you get to the car by the time I count to 5?" (Just be sure to count slowly.)

★ **Buckling up the car seat:**

- Make up a song about buckling up. You might sing, "This is the way we buckle up…" (to the tune of "This is the way we wash our clothes").

- Show him a picture of himself safely buckled in his seat. Keep it in his travel book.

- Encourage your child to help with "buckling up" as much as he is able. He could pull the strap over his shoulders and then it is Mommy's turn to do the rest. You might say, "Shayna's turn. Please, help me with the straps. Mommy's turn. Snap. Snap. All done."

- State the rule that the car cannot go until everybody has their seatbelts on.

Tip: Make your car a child-friendly place.

If your child is busy in the car, both you and he will have a happier experience.

★ **Many parents have found it successful to have an activity bin in the car.** Fill the activity bin with a few of your child's favorite things. Some examples might be a couple of books, markers and drawing paper, figurines, or a sticker book. You can create a bin by using any box or plastic, lidded container. Keep the bin in the car, but change the contents every week. By changing the toys, the bin is always interesting and fun for your child. Another option is to use a backseat organizer. These hang from the front seat headrest and contain compartments for storing toys, CDs, drinks/snacks, or the travel book. Some have mirrors to entertain younger children.

★ **Children's music CDs:** There are many music CDs that have music and lyrics that both you and your child will enjoy. You'll find some with songs from your child's favorite television shows and movies. There are also music CDs that have songs with a school readiness focus that offer your child a fun way to learn how to count, say the letters, or learn how to rhyme, etc. Some CDs include songs about riding in the car (Sesame Street/Bert & Ernie, Going Riding in the Car) or everyday routines such as dressing, brushing teeth, etc. You and your child will have the opportunity to sing, laugh and learn together. This is a great way to make your ride to places enjoyable for you and your child.

3

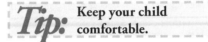

Tip: Provide your child choices.

Use choices to prevent challenging behavior. When you offer your child a choice, you provide him with the opportunity to have control and be independent.

* **If your child has limited communication skills, provide him with a choice board.** These are pictured choices from which he can tell you what he wants. They could be photos or clip art. You might have a page in his travel book of song choices, CD choices, or snack/drink choices, etc. Each picture can be velcroed onto a page in his travel book and he can point to the picture or give it to you to indicate his choice. For children who have vision impairments or blindness, you can offer a choice by handing your child two objects or pieces of objects and asking the child to make a selection.

* **Let your child choose the music to be played.** You might like country music but it might not be his choice. Listen to it another time when you are in the car alone. A pleasant ride running errands will make listening to the Wiggles or a Raffi CD one more time well worth the effort. You might even enjoy singing with your child. Most children love this activity.

* **Some families have DVD players and hand-held game systems for the car.** These are passive activities that don't promote learning or building a relationship with your child. You might want to save these for those

longer trips. Running errands are a great opportunity to interact with your child, create a pleasurable routine, and help your child learn.

Tip: Keep your child comfortable.

Make sure that your child is not too hot or cold. If he has limited language, he may not be able to tell you that he is uncomfortable (except through challenging behavior). If you can, cool the car off in advance. If your child has a voice output device, program "I'm hot" and "I'm cold" into it so he can let you how he feels. Have a comfort object (e.g., blankie) in the car for comfort and warmth. If your child has a special comfort item or toy, it will pay to keep a duplicate in the car so you aren't looking for it at the last minute as you are trying to leave the house.

These simple prevention tips can make getting in the car or on the bus to run errands much easier for your child. Once out of the house, you and your child can take care of these household tasks and have fun during your time together.

In closing, please remember that the team of professionals that support you and your child will have additional specific ideas about how to help your child. Don't forget to ask them! Your child's speech therapist, physical therapist, teacher, or other professional should be able to help you think about the best way to support your child within daily routines and community activities. If your child is having persistent challenging behavior within this activity, you should ask the professionals who work with you to help develop a behavior support plan that will provide more specific strategies to prevent challenging behavior and help your child develop new social and communication skills.

Technical Assistance Center on Social Emotional Intervention for Young Children
www.challengingbehavior.org

This document is public domain and may be reproduced without permission.
Reproduction of this document is strongly encouraged.
Developed in collaboration with PACER Center (Parent Advocacy Coalition for Educational Rights)

UNIVERSITY OF
SOUTH FLORIDA

4

Making Life Easier: **Running Errands**

* Use a **transition warning** (e.g., verbal, timer, count down, sing a song).

* **Tell** your child where you will be going.
  * Use "First..., Then..." statements.
  * Use a Travel Book.
  * Include one of your child's favorite places.
  * Provide a transition object (toy, blankie, book, travel book, etc.).
  * Provide 2 or 3 choices for the transition object.

* Prepare a **cooler**.

* Prepare your **diaper bag** or a backpack (written list in bag).

* Getting in the **Car Seat**:
  * Make getting to the car a game (sing, skip, hop, race, count to 10).

* Make buckling up in his car a game (sing, encourage child's your child's help).

* Show a picture of him safely buckled in his seat. Keep it in his travel book.

* Insist that everybody has their seatbelts on before the car moves.

* Provide your child **choices**.
  * Your child could choose music, toys, books, etc.

* Make **your car** a "child friendly" place.
  * Keep an activity bin in the car. Rotate the contents every now and then. Allow your child to choose some of the contents.
  * Play children's music CDs. Provide 2 or 3 choices. Sing together.
  * Cool or heat car in advance. Provide a means for your child to communicate how he feels.

Making Life Easier

By Pamelazita Buschbacher, Ed.D.   Illustrated by Sarah I. Payton

Holidays: Strategies for Success

While the holiday season is filled with enjoyable activities, events and traditions, it can also be a hectic and stressful time. Travel, shopping, loud music, bright lights, unfamiliar food, and busy schedules can turn typical routines upside down! The disruption to routine can be particularly difficult for children who depend on routine and predictability to engage in appropriate behavior.

The following tips will help ensure that the holiday season is enjoyable for you and your child.

Tip: **Prepare your child for changes.**

Talk to your child about changes to the schedule and environment. Look at pictures from previous holidays and talk about what happened during those events. Also talk about this year's special programs and about behavior expectations, e.g., "we will sit and listen quietly during the presentation...when the program is over, we will go to the lobby and have some cookies and punch." Discuss upcoming trips several days before the departure date. Let your child know when you will be leaving, where you will be going, and what you will do while away. Repeat these conversations several times before traveling.

1

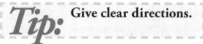 **Involve your child in preparations and minimize surprises.**

If you are going to decorate the house or bake special goodies, involve your child and make the tasks fun! It could be upsetting for your child to come home from school to find the home looking very different with unfamiliar items and things out of place. Take decorations out gradually and allow your child to explore them so that she has time to adjust to the changes.

Pace your holiday activities.

Busy holiday calendars can leave adults and children worn out and stressed. When possible, balance times of high activity with calm, relaxed times. Try to spread activities out over the holiday season.

★ **Keep aspects of your typical routine whenever possible.** Consistency and familiarity can help build coping skills for the unfamiliar. As much as possible, preserve bedtimes and other routines. Allow for a leisurely bath, story, song or cuddle. Eat meals together.

★ **Plan for a regular 'Quiet Time'.** Try to build in time each day to provide your child with activities that she finds soothing or relaxing.

★ **Don't shop 'til you drop.** If your holiday season involves lots of shopping or errands, think carefully about how to involve your child. Stores will look and feel different this time of year as they are often extremely crowded and noisy. Children may become frightened or overwhelmed. Consider making trips brief, shopping at less crowded times, or leaving your child with another caregiver. If you have errands to run, limit the number of places you visit and let your child know that the errands will end at a fun place for her (e.g., a park, playground, ice cream store, etc.).

Give clear directions.

Give your child a positive direction that assumes she will cooperate. For example, instead of saying "Amy, do you want to get on the plane?" it is better to say, "Oh look, it's time to walk onto the plane. 1-2-3-4-5, Let's go." Remind her of expectations. For example, you might say, "Remember, walking feet on the plane." It is also helpful to show your child the behavior using pictures or by modeling it yourself.

★ **Use Positive Words.** Clearly and simply state what you expect your child to do instead of what not to do. Encourage your child in a way that lets her know that she is exhibiting the desired behavior.

★ **Give warnings that change is coming.** Most young children need help transitioning from one activity to another, especially if they are engaged in an activity that they enjoy. Let your child know in advance that a change is coming. Give a few staggered warnings letting her know how much time is left in the current activity as well as what is coming up next. Help your child through the transition by talking to her or singing a song such as "The Clean-Up Song" or adapting a familiar song to the task.

2

★ **Use 'Wait Time'.** A wait time of about 4 to 20 seconds is often all that is needed for a child to process and respond to a request.

★ **Provide choices, whenever possible.** Providing limited choices (two or three) for a child in a difficult situation can be a powerful strategy in preventing challenging behavior and redirecting a child to more acceptable behavior and cooperation. Choices help give children a sense of control over their surroundings and activities while still doing what needs to be done! Be sure that ALL the choices you offer are helping reach that goal! For example, if it is time to get dressed ask your child if she wants to get dressed by herself or with your help.

★ **Provide frequent and specific praise.** Let your child know when she is being cooperative and helpful by praising her specifically for what she is doing. For example, you might give your child a high five for sitting quietly in the car or you might say, "Thank you for holding my hand in the parking lot."

★ **Empathize with your child's feelings.** If your child cries, hits, bites, screams or hides, provide an emotional label for how she might be feeling and reassure her. Avoid punishment (e.g. "If you don't sit still, I am going to spank you.") and negative, and usually, untrue comments "Big girls don't cry" or "There is nothing to be afraid of." Let your child cry and comfort her by hugging, patting and/or using a soothing touch.

Tip: Prepare family and friends.

Inform family and friends of helpful strategies. Talk to your family and friends about strategies that might help ensure your child's success before spending time together. Consider specific aspects or situations that might have a negative impact on your child's behavior (e.g., sensory issues, difficulty waiting, food allergies or sensitivities, etc.) and share strategies that have worked for you. Be sure to focus on your child's strengths and strategies for success.

Tip: Pack for success!

When your holiday plans include time away from home, bring familiar items, activities and foods with you. Pack activity bags that include favorite books, toys, and games. If possible, have your child help pack the bags so she can choose a few of the items herself. You might say, "Brianna, do you want to take Mickey Mouse or blankie in your bag?" This gives her a feeling of control and supports her growing sense of confidence and sense of competency.

For many families the holidays are a time of feasting and enjoying all kinds of yummy treats. Be attentive to diet changes and how they may affect your child. Chocolate, caffeine, sugar, and dairy products may have an impact of your child's digestion, well-being, and behavior. If your child follows a particular diet, be sure to bring items with you that might not be available where you are going. Pack nutritious food and drink options to balance out sweet, holiday treats.

Tip: Pre-travel planning.

★ **Reassure your child.** Let your child know that you will be with her and that she can take along a favorite toy or blanket. For example you might say, "Daddy will be with you" or "You can hold blankie on the plane."

★ **Rest stops aren't just for resting.** Familiarize yourself with your travel route as well as with parks and rest areas along the way. These offer great opportunities for children to run, jump, play with a ball, blow bubbles, and stretch. Many family-friendly restaurants and airports have play spaces also. A good rule is to take a ten minute break every two hours.

3

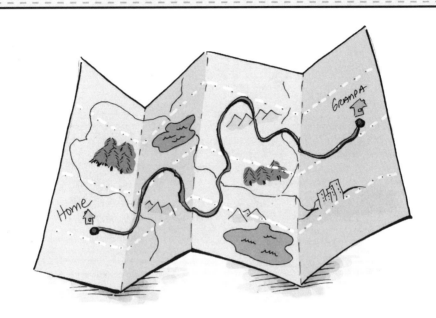

★ **Create a personal picture story about the trip.** Create a small book with photos of the airport and plane or of the bus depot, bus, car or train. As you read the book with your child, let her know what will happen and how you expect her to behave. Read this to your child several times before the trip. Also, make sure to bring it along as a reminder. When children understand what is going to happen, they are less anxious which can increase cooperation and reduce challenging behavior.

 Tip: Celebrate the successes along the way.

In closing, please remember that the team of professionals that support you and your child will have additional specific ideas about how to help your child. Don't forget to ask them! Your child's speech and language therapist, physical therapist, occupational therapist, teacher, or other professional should be able to help you think about the best way to support your child over the holiday season. They are usually more than willing to help you make any needed specific supports (for example, a Travel Book, a Waiting Bag, a personal picture story, etc.). If your child is having persistent challenging behavior, you should ask the professionals who work with you to help develop a behavior support plan that will provide more specific strategies to prevent challenging behavior and help your child develop new social and communication skills.

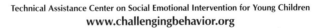

Technical Assistance Center on Social Emotional Intervention for Young Children
www.challengingbehavior.org

IDEAs that Work

This document is public domain and may be reproduced without permission.
Reproduction of this document is strongly encouraged.
Developed in collaboration with PACER Center (Parent Advocacy Coalition for Educational Rights)

USF
UNIVERSITY OF
SOUTH FLORIDA

4

Making Life Easier: Surviving and Enjoying the Holidays

★ **Prepare your child for changes** in routines and schedule.

★ **Involve your child** in some of the holiday preparations.

★ Keep aspects of your **typical routine** whenever possible.

★ Give **clear directions**.
  - Use **positive words**.
  - Provide **transition warnings**.
  - Use **'Wait Time.'**
  - Provide limited **choices**.
  - Tell your child **how to behave**.
  - Provide **frequent and specific praise** for acceptable behavior.

★ **Empathize** with your child's feelings.

★ **Inform family** and friends of helpful strategies.

★ Be attentive to **your child's diet**.

★ Holiday Travel – **Plan ahead**
  - Pack a bag of **favorite items** to take with you.
  - Call airlines, airport or bus depot ahead about **special accommodations**.
  - **Visit the airport** or bus depot in advance.
  - Create a **personal story**.

★ **Celebrate** the successes along the way.

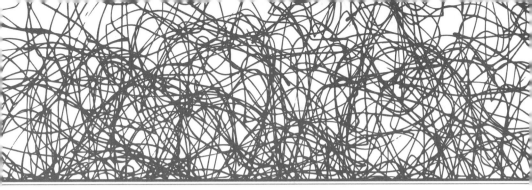

About the Authors

Jim Forgan and Mary Anne Richey have spent a combined 52 years working with children with executive functioning difficulties and ADHD in school settings, in private practice, and at home. The first thing you need to know about the authors is that each is the parent of a child with ADHD and executive functioning difficulty.

Jim Forgan, Ph.D., is an associate professor and Licensed School Psychologist. He teaches others how to teach and assess children with ADHD, executive functioning difficulty, and other types of learning disabilities at Florida Atlantic University. In private practice, he works with families of children with ADHD, EF, and other learning differences. Jim consults with public and private schools doing workshops on ADHD, executive functioning, dyslexia, problem solving, and accommodations for learning disabilities. You may reach him at http://www.JimForgan.com.

Mary Anne Richey, M.Ed., is a Licensed School Psychologist in a private practice providing evaluation of children with learning differences, consultations in private and public schools, and workshops on ADHD, executive functioning difficulties, and gifted students. She also has experience as a middle school teacher, administrator, high school guidance counselor, and adjunct college instructor. In 2013, she was honored as School Psychologist of the Year by the Florida Association of School Psychologists and was a nominee for the 2014 National

School Psychologist of the Year chosen by the National Association of School Psychologists.

Throughout this book, Jim and Mary Anne help parents manage the issues they face and incorporate strategies to help their children succeed in school and life. They have presented at national conventions and workshops for parents and professionals on strategies for helping those with ADHD and executive functioning difficulties maximize their potential. They are coauthors of *Raising Boys With ADHD* and *Raising Girls With ADHD*. They share an integrated perspective on ADHD and executive functioning based on their experiences as parents and professionals, their academic research, and their interactions with so many other parents raising girls and boys with executive functioning difficulty and ADHD.